LIVERPOOL
THE WORLD IN ONE CITY
A JOURNALIST'S VIEW OF LIVERPOOL

This book is dedicated to my wife, Alison, our son Cameron, and to the memory of my mother, Margaret Ancell Charters.

© David Charters 2003
Published by The Bluecoat Press, Liverpool
Book design by March Design, Liverpool
Photographs courtesy of Liverpool Daily Post and Echo
Printed by The Universities Press, Belfast

ISBN 1 904438 10 5

Acknowledgments

I should like to thank all my friends and colleagues, past and present, at the *Daily Post*, without whose patience and kindness this book could not have been published. My special thanks go to our wonderful team of photographers whose images so often say more than the words. No book of this kind could be written without the co-operation and sympathy of the people being featured. I've met only kindness and understanding in my meetings with them. I am also very grateful to Ron Formby, editor of the *Scottie Press*, and all his friends in the Vauxhall History and Heritage Group who have always helped me with my researches. Last but not least, my thanks go to Frances Gleeson who edited this collection, and to everyone at The Bluecoat Press for all their encouragement and assistance.

LIVERPOOL
THE WORLD IN ONE CITY
A JOURNALIST'S VIEW OF LIVERPOOL

DAVID CHARTERS

CONTENTS

FOREWORD

I have been a journalist writing about Merseyside for more than 40 years, from the first sprouting of whiskers on my chin, to the greying of what remains of my hair. In this time I have written many thousands of stories, numbering millions of words.

The newspaper writer stands on the brink of history. He is there to form his thoughts into sentences that he hopes will capture the moment, through the mood of the people, their hopes and their fears.

This is not a history book in the formal sense. These stories are selections from our region's past, snapshots capturing a fleeting moment. The intention of this book is to give the reader an idea of how it was when something momentous happened, or was about to happen – to be in the company of someone involved in those events, to be in the place where they happened. The pieces in this collection are moments frozen in time.

All the stories are drawn from articles originally published in the *Daily Post* where I have worked since 1988. Much of the material reflects the past and draws on the humour, the sorrow, the emotions, and the recollections of the people who lived those days, from young promise to the stoop of experience.

In my opinion, good journalistic writing always places people first. My job has been to find the people and write about them, it is as simple as that. People are central to all good newspaper stories. Some I liked and some I didn't, but all were interesting.

To most of us, newspapers come and go in a day. But if you were the person being written about, you would judge it differently. Then the article becomes a record of your own life. I can think of no finer compliment than to see something I have written being pasted in a scrapbook. Even as a cub reporter in Birkenhead, I was driven by that thought. Unfailingly, you should give of your best, because the man reading the paper on the bus deserves no less.

For me, writing has been a great privilege. There could be nothing finer than telling the stories of people. All our lives are driven by stories. They take us from the knees of our mothers and fathers to the grand libraries, by way of comics, cinema, theatre, as well as the crackling firesides of Christmas. I hope this book persuades you that newspaper writing can be part of that grand tradition.

David Charters 2003

THE FAMOUS
(AND THE INFAMOUS)

ALL THAT JAZZ: GEORGE MELLY

George Melly lives in London now, but he often returns to his childhood home of Liverpool. I have met him on two occasions, in 1998 and 2001, and thoroughly enjoyed his convivial conversation. He has the voice of a heavy trifle, rich and moist, which, in moments of high emotion, sinks deep into the blues mud of the Mississippi Delta. His generously filled lips with very little prompting spread into a smile, celebrating the absurdity of human kind.

Maybe that's why George Melly was standing, magnificently, in a purple suit and a blue hat on a quayside, beneath a lamp whose glow stretched along the damp cobbles of dusk. Here, portly and true, with a silver pin securing the band to his hat, was that rare creature: a Liverpudlian who does not attribute his fame to an upbringing in which wit and understanding were flinted on poverty and bitterness. Melly – jazz and blues singer, writer, wearer of hats (the most recent being of Peruvian origin), striped jackets and spats, admirer of surrealistic art and a raconteur who can make even an appearance on a TV chat show enjoyable – was the son of the upper middle classes.

Born to Francis Heywood and Edith Maud Melly and kept by shipping wealth in a large Victorian house on the fringes of Sefton Park, the young George was sent to Stowe public school before he joined the Royal Navy. He served as an able seaman from 1944-47, gathering some material for his autobiography, *Rum, Bum and Concertina*.

He came immediately before that generation, led by Peter Cook and Richard Ingrams, whose observations on the brittle nature of authority and life in high society began the satire boom. To some extent, George was a mentor of these younger men, writing the captions for the Flook cartoon strip by Trog (Wally Fawkes), which appeared in the *Daily Mail* from 1956-71. In fact, for many, George's book, *Revolt into Style*, was the definitive work about the 1960s. Its emphasis was on how youthful exuberance could be tamed and re-branded in a blander form by people with power and money.

In his home there had been a libertarian atmosphere. That helped open his feelings to the many possibilities in life, all of which should be experienced unconstrained by the gloomy conventions of others. Of course there was sex – straddling both sides of the sofa in about equal measure; boozing – on a grand scale to match Brendan Behan or F Scott Fitzgerald, but with lashings more pleasure; song – a great and glorious swelling of notes from somewhere within; and jokes, mimicry, sorrows, love and sympathy.

I mention the Irish writer Behan, the Borstal boy famed for *The Hostage* and *The Queer Fellow*, who burst into the literary circles of London and New York in the late 1950s with all the delicacy of assault and battery.

"I did bump into him from time to time, but I would try to avoid him if I saw him coming," says George. "He was always so drunk. But I failed to avoid him once on the Fulham Road early one morning. Well, when I say early, I mean I had gone to my pub at eleven o'clock, and there he was singing Irish rebel songs, awfully out of tune, until he was ejected by the owner whom, I may say, came from Dublin. But he was a wonderful writer, with no discipline, who needed Joan Littlewood (the stage director) to lick it into shape, but it was wonderful."

Rather foolishly, I suggest that his brother Dominic, the folk singer and writer, could out-drink Brendan, but enjoyed longer periods of sobriety.

"Did he? Well, I must have met him in one of his drunken periods," replies George. "It was at the BBC in a programme called *Late Night Line-Up*, which was known among us as 'Late Night Booze-Up' because its hospitality was always open. God, he was drunk! He insisted on two things. The first one was he thought that some perfectly harmless lackey of the BBC was upper-class and he kept trying to kick him, missing each time. The other was that he was convinced that I, as a Liverpudlian, had been running around the city with my arse hanging out of my breeks. I couldn't persuade him that I had had a middle-class upbringing and had my arse well within my breeks."

Dylan Thomas? Had he met the Welshman with a fondness for the bottle?

"Only once, for an evening," says George. "He kept falling on tables and things. I admired him as a poet, but I don't know what he was like as a human being, only as a drink receptacle."

It was a world into which the young George fitted with ease. He said, "I always felt part of it. I never felt naive in it."

His favourite haunt remains the Colony Room, in the Soho Club, once run by the extraordinary Muriel Belcher, which attracted what could be generously described as the Bohemian set. "These days," he says, "the Colony Room is full of the Brit Pack – Damien Hirst, Tracey Emin. They go there a lot, I think, because they truly revere Francis Bacon. He drank there for many years, and it is a kind of shrine. The booze was very important for many of them, but not all. Francis drank up a storm. Lucian Freud drank less."

Wasn't it a wonder that people managed to function at all, particularly after the lunch-time sessions?

"I don't think they did much! Francis painted from the small hours until lunch-time," replies George. But are the young people of today having as much fun? "How can one tell?" he says. "As one gets older, one takes a golden brush to the past, but a lot of it was probably boring and miserable. The good bits were very good, though."

He regrets the demise of the extended lunch, so familiar to the journalists of his day.

"This lot may be very fit on their rotten vegetables and exercise, but they are not having the fun," he says.

As a gesture to the new age, George, who lives with his wife Diana, has given up cigarettes. "I had terrible bronchitis and had to. I regret it, but I really almost died from a lack of oxygen," he says, recalling a spell in hospital. George also affects a little deafness these days and a hearing aid can be spotted among the tufts around his left ear, bringing some mercy to the raw tonsils of his companions, but his conversation flows just the same.

Revolt into Style, published 30 years ago, tells how the rebels of rock were tamed by the show-biz establishment. In this book, Melly suggested that, with the Beatles' LP *Sergeant Pepper's Lonely Hearts' Club Band*, pop had reached its zenith. Was that still true?

"I think it is. I think that whole period of the nineteen sixties and the early nineteen seventies was much better than it is now, although one is not really in a position to judge. I was just young enough then. Above all with rock music, you have to be young. You listen to Sergeant Pepper's or the early Stones rather like one's grandfather listened to Harry Lauder. It's part of one's youth. But everything now is 'retro' – even yesterday afternoon is revived! Like early jazz, which was a thing born of itself, nothing like it had existed before, you could see its roots – same with rhythm and blues and pop. They are all so highly developed, and they developed through human beings, whereas now it's drum machines. In a sense, I suppose, the Beatles started it off with their producer, George Martin, who added things. But there, the result was extraordinary, a wonderful record.

"Oasis, for instance, is a pleasant enough noise – unlike the people who make it, who seem extremely unpleasant! – but it is very retro-Beatles as far as I can hear. I don't know what's original now. Punk was original. It was unbearable, musically, but at least it was a positive thing after all that loud super-starism of the late nineteen seventies."

Was there a danger that studio technology could kill the link between youth and music, both in a romantic and a story-telling form?

"You see," he says, "the fat cats of the music industry have always been keen to turn this into cash as quick as they could, but they did meet with a certain resistance at one time. I am not sure they do now. I was talking to Ian Drury (who has since died) the other day. He's a wonderful man. He has never compromised and what he does is terrifically original. The Kinks were a great band for that reason. They actually invented their own world and projected it. But there is a predictable blandness in the albums I listen to now, only in passing, never deliberately.

Melly still sings regularly at venues across the country with John Chilton's Feetwarmers. I ask him why did he like the black blues so much?

"Ah," (and here you must try and imagine the depth and smoke and hooch in the Melly voice when it ponders and then savours a point), "because it was the best. Still is. I fell in love with Bessie Smith, the great blues singer, in nineteen forty-four. I am just as much in love with her now as I was then."

11

Do you think white men can sing the blues?

"I think they can sing it a bit. I mean, I try," he says. "But I would never say they can sing it like a black man. They don't have the black experience. But I think they can sing jazz songs."

What does he think of his native city now?

"Liverpool will always be Liverpool and that's for sure. I love the fact that they're restoring the old Georgian houses instead of knocking them down. The spirit seems to be pretty much the same, but I never understand why they say Liverpool people whinge. Birmingham people whinge. Liverpool people are usually very cheerful. Even when they're depressed, they're funny."

Maybe that was how George Melly, who is now walking into the night in his hat, found the blues.

LORD HAW HAW'S LIVERPOOL DAYS

As Fascism attempts to emerse again in Europe, it is important
not to forget its origins. This article first appeared in March 2002.

~

To the modern eye, he was an unimpressive figure in a murky hall: short and thin, with a sheen of sweat on his pale, brooding face that nodded and jerked above his black shirt. Sometimes, when he turned to the lights that hung above the Union Flag on the table, you could see the scar that ran from his right ear all the way to the tight curves of his mouth. He said it was a duelling wound, but there were doubters.

These were good days for insignificant little men with big ideas who wanted to make their way in the world. Benito Mussolini and Adolf Hitler had shown what could be done if only you had the will. And then there was this William Joyce, a familiar figure in the halls and pubs of Liverpool, where he was trying to gain support for Oswald Mosley and his British Union of Fascists, who wore black shirts just like the Fascisti in Italy.

Joyce's favoured stomping ground was around the Great Homer Street area of the city, but his spirit was zealous and he would travel anywhere to draw people to the cause. His meeting at Wallasey Town Hall on 24 January 1937 wasn't much of a success. Fewer than a hundred people turned up, and some of them were sheltering from the cold. The British didn't seem to accept the message like Hitler's Nazis and Mussolini's people, who held massive rallies with lots of banners and goose-stepping and songs. The reception at Wavertree Town Hall was more promising. Joyce gave his usual diatribe against the Jews and the Communists and a large crowd listened for more than an hour without interruption.

Like Mosley, Goebbels, and many others attracted to extreme politics, Joyce was a man of ability who found it difficult to settle in mainstream society. He was born to Michael and Gertrude Joyce on 24 April 1906 in a three-storey house of brownstone in Herkimer Street, Brooklyn, New York. His mother had been raised in Yorkshire, but his father was from County Galway. The family soon returned to Ireland, where Michael served with the Royal Irish Constabulary. On the establishment of the Irish Free State, they moved to Clapham, London, where Michael was appointed general manager of a store.

Slight of build, around 5ft 4in tall and neat in appearance, young Joyce, who had benefited greatly from an education under the Jesuits, was a bright fellow. He was just 17 when he joined the British Union of Fascists, which was led by the towering figure of Mosley. A mesmeric orator and former member of the Labour Government, Mosley enjoyed considerable support in the Press and amongst the aristocracy, as well as the disillusioned.

To the delight of his parents, Joyce gained a place at London University where he was awarded a first-class honours degree in literature, leading to the popular papers dubbing him, 'the Professor of Fascism'. After that, he did a post-graduate course in German philology and psychology.

The family, including Joyce's four brothers and one sister, moved around a lot. When they were based in Oldham, Joyce made an application to join London University's Officer Training Corps, expressing his sense of nationalism in fervent terms.

I am prepared to draw the sword in British interests. I have always been desirous of devoting all the loyalty and energy I possess to the country I love so dearly.

During this time, Joyce, who had now married, made a living from teaching, then he set up his own correspondence school. This gave him time to devote his attention to his growing interest in politics, discovering that an argument could be driven home by violence as well as intellect. In fact, that 'duelling' scar was not caused by the cut of a rapier in a Heidelberg garden, but by the slash of a razor in Manchester, when the Fascists and the Communists had a battle. At another riot in Carlisle, Joyce was struck on the head by a passing chair leg. He was comforted by Margaret ('Margot') White, another member of the British Union of Fascists, who was brought up in Cheetham Hill, Manchester. Already separated from his first wife, Joyce fell in love. The couple married. Margot had friends on Merseyside who were visited by her and Joyce as they pursued their Fascist mission. Wallasey and New Brighton were certainly known to them, as would be heard later in his broadcasts.

Joyce was Mosley's director of propaganda and a persuasive orator in his own right. However, shortly after Joyce's address at Wallasey Town Hall, the two men fell out over Joyce's ambition for closer links with Hitler's Germany. This was

Joyce's moment. He began his own party, the British National Socialist League. Soon he was living in a luxurious flat in South Kensington in London and producing *The Helmsman* magazine. It seems likely that his funding came from Dr Joseph Goebbels, Hitler's propaganda minister.

Five weeks before the start of war, Joyce and Margot (who enjoyed sucking her cigarettes from a long holder in the style of a Hollywood gossip columnist) had left for Germany, settling in a small flat in Berlin. Joyce was a skilled propagandist. His 'Jairmany calling' broadcasts were issued with the insouciant drawl of a cad introducing himself to a chorus girl, but the messages were cunning and designed to undermine British morale.

Joyce exposed the country's class differences during the Blitz by saying some of Liverpool's anti-aircraft cover had been transferred to London to defend Churchill and the royal family. Margot also gave broadcasts and was nicknamed Lady Haw Haw. It was Joyce's remarkable knowledge of local geography that worried his listeners. Before an attack on Liverpool, he said, "We shall spread Hartley's jam on Crawford's cream crackers." He warned the people of New Brighton that the Luftwaffe would be paying attention to Warren Drive and, "that promenade of yours".

His most infamous broadcast was made from Hamburg a few hours before Germany's surrender. Burping repeatedly and slurring his words, the drunken Haw Haw spoke of how he wished Britain and Germany could have united to counter the Communist menace from the East.

At the end of May 1945, Joyce was shot in the thigh and captured by British soldiers in a wood at Flensburg, near the German/Danish frontier. He was tried as a traitor at the Old Bailey. In his defence, he claimed to be an American who had adopted German nationality before the USA entered the war, therefore he could not have betrayed Britain. But it was discovered on passport applications that Joyce had declared himself to be a British subject.

At 9am on 3 January 1946, he was hanged in Wandsworth Prison. He was 39. The authorities said he died with dignity.

Margot was held in a detainment camp in Germany until 3 January 1948. In 1976, Lord Haw Haw's daughter, Heather Joyce, successfully applied for his body to be exhumed from Wandsworth Cemetery and reburied in Galway. Perhaps, in the end, Joyce was the 'patriot' who couldn't find a country.

THE DEATH OF GEORGE HARRISON

George Harrison died on 29 November 2001. This article, which formed part of a tribute to George, was published on 1 December 2001, after news of his death was announced publicly.

~

Lovers and losers, the mighty and the poor of the world, were yesterday listening to the songs of the bus driver's son, who gave everyone a memory, a time to smile. That was his gift to us.

And the prime ministers, the presidents, and the money-rollers of show business, bustled and strained to have their tributes to him read on TV and radio. Flags drooped at half-mast and the Queen issued a statement ... but he had a keen sense of humour, George Harrison of the Beatles. Some say that, in a contest of wit, he could easily match his angry and exuberant pal, John Lennon. After all, you had to be able to laugh a bit at life when your window, in the back bedroom of a terraced house, overlooked the privy in the yard.

Yesterday, reporters with foreign accents and fluffy-headed microphones were striding by the nine houses on the right side of Arnold Grove, Wavertree, on the outskirts of Liverpool, where old-fashioned people still hang baskets of flowers on the painted brick walls of their homes. The news boys and girls were hoping that somebody would say something that would explain the life of the guitarist, whose face, with the quizzical-brown eyes and high cheekbones, was once clasped in the lockets of millions of girls.

Now, only Ivy Andrews, from number one, remembers George, running up and down the street, grazing his knees, crying for a moment, and then forgetting it, like all the other little boys. She has been on the street on the opposite side to the Harrisons' old house, for almost 60 years. It was here she raised her own three children. She is 82 now, and it all seems a long time ago, though the journalists, just strangers to her, kept asking questions.

News of George's death was spreading around the city. The Union Flag was hanging at half-mast over Liverpool Town Hall, where a book of condolence had just opened. People were stopping each other to exchange memories. Nearly everyone has a favourite Beatles' song, one that was special to them when they were younger. Often it was George's *Something*, or *Here Comes The Sun*.

The mood wasn't quite the same as it was on 8 December 1980. That had been sudden. John was shot down in his prime. We all knew George would die soon, but that didn't lessen the sense of sorrow. He was held in just as much affection, perhaps more, but feelings can be expressed quietly. That was George's style, even though he had worn a canary-yellow waistcoat to the Liverpool Institute High School, risking the wrath of the head, Jake 'The Baz' Edwards, whose cane had a mean swish. But then George was posing as a rock 'n' roll rebel with grease in his hair. Lessons didn't count for much.

He was born to Harry and Louise at number 12 Arnold Grove, on 25 February 1943, the youngest of their children, arriving after Louise, Harry and Peter. "Every door here was open then," said Ivy. "It wasn't a hush-hush grove. There were lots of children and they used to trot in here. I was Ivy to everyone."

George and the family left the house when he was about seven. Yesterday, a 63-year-old Kathleen Hughes was peeping behind the black front-door. She came here in 1962, completely unaware that this little street would become a place of pilgrimage.

"More and more people come every year," she said, referring particularly to the open-topped buses that carry tourists to the haunts of the Beatles. "Some of them knock on the door and want to take photographs. I don't let them in. Sometimes there are so many I can't get in and out with my shopping. George lived in the back bedroom. They are only two-up, two-down, these houses. He must have shared the bedroom with the other children, you did in those days. There was no inside bathroom then, just an outside loo."

As she spoke, George's unmistakable wailing guitar could be heard on car radios at the top of the road. Those sounds were also being heard in the world's great cities. In Los Angeles, where he died, tributes were laid on George's star on the Hollywood Walk of Fame. Religious leaders were speaking of his sense of peace. This was George the mystic, who placed human love as the highest attainment.

It had been a long journey for the handsome little boy whose proud mother Louise used to watch him practising Chuck Berry riffs on his first guitar. As dusk settled, fans from many countries converged on Mathew Street, home of The Cavern. Flowers were left at the foot of the Wall of Fame, which features the name of every group and solo performer to have appeared at the club, including, of course, the Beatles. There are always ironies in life, and, as George was dying on Thursday night, Tom Robinson was making his debut at The Cavern. It promised to be one of the happiest occasions in the career of the man whose own hits include *2468 Motorway* and *War Child*. A brick inscribed with his name was to be laid in the wall.

"Any joyfulness that you might have felt at finally being part of this great mass of history is tempered by the sombre day that has dawned," said Tom, who is 51. "I was on stage at The Cavern when he died. Yes, as he died, me and my guys were on the stage. We didn't know that then. The news had not come through.

"To have lost fifty per cent of the greatest group of all time with premature deaths is so sad. I met him twice through Elton John. He was a sweet, unassuming man, who met you with complete dignity as a human being. He didn't pull any airs and graces or star numbers. I don't think, judging by his career, demeanour and song writing since the Beatles, that he was at all interested in the fame machine. He was more interested in the spiritual dimension. It was more important to him than fame, power, money, or music. But he did make the finest post-Beatles song, *When We Was Fab*.

"The whole Beatles generation, which is us, have all grown older and are no longer as fab as we thought ourselves in the sixties. When I met George he was with Billy Connolly and they were wise-cracking away. I was in awe, really." Just down the street, was Billy Kinsley of the Merseybeats, who had a string of successful records in the sixties. "I loved him in a lot of ways," he added. "I have known him since I was fourteen. Seeing the Beatles changed my life. They were the best group ever. George was very limited as a guitar player to begin with. But he became one of the greatest guitarists in the world. He was devoted to his music."

Last night, the Merseybeats were performing in Skegness and they ended the show with their hit *Sorrow*. George loved the song. Its opening line, 'With your long blonde hair and eyes of blue', reminded him of his first wife, Patti Boyd.

Just behind Billy Kinsley, they were taking down the poster advertising Tom Robinson's concert. Soon they would be billing the next act. Perhaps George was right about fame.

The message on the flowers below read:

RIP, George, now with Your Sweet Lord. John will welcome you with open arms. From everybody from The Cavern and fans across the world.

And the girls were walking towards Mathew Street last night, smelling again the fruit in the boxes outside the warehouses. They remembered how it was, when they were young, and George Harrison had the face of an angel.

GEORGE HARRISON'S LAST VISIT TO THE CAVERN CLUB

Five years before his death in 2001, George Harrison returned to Mathew Street, home of the Cavern Club. As a tribute, this article recalls a chance meeting between the man himself and Chris Hockenhull, founder and chairman of the Dylan Merseyside Fan Club.

~

It was cold and the drizzle was deepening the red of the bricks, which had been laid, some years back, in a zig-zag pattern over the old cobbles. There is a certain mood on a street in the weeks just before Christmas and that's how it was on this evening, with the rasp of rapid steps, the brushing of shoulders, and eyes staring into the dusk. Collars were high and hats were pulled down low. So stood the man outside the shop in the lamp light, and he seemed bewildered, looking up and down the way, a little sunken in his great black coat and scarf. With him was a lady, not quite five feet high, but very elegant, and her arm was linked in his. "Is there a place where you can get a drink round here?" asked the man, as he was joined by another in the shop doorway.

It was almost exactly five years ago when George Harrison was back on Mathew Street, home of the Cavern Club, nosing in some of the old haunts with his Mexican wife, Olivia. This was the man that the German girls called the 'beautiful one', who stood on the left of the stage and bent his knees before raising the guitar for his solo breaks in the songs the Beatles performed at the Star Club, Hamburg.

Now he was 53 and the smile from those warm brown eyes that had stared from a million posters, and his distinctive high cheekbones, were not so familiar. For a blink or two, the other man in the doorway didn't recognise his questioner. But moments earlier, Harrison had heard the man talking about Bob Dylan, which was a little unexpected in the Beatles Shop.

This was the strange meeting of Harrison, a close friend of Dylan, and Chris Hockenhull, founder and chairman of the Dylan Merseyside fan club. Just seconds before, Harrison had been in the shop, smiling at the souvenirs, a quarter of which were dedicated to him. Japanese fans, cheeping away in an excited fashion, had been pointing their camcorders at everything in sight, except the man in the hat and coat.

"I wasn't aware that he had been in the same place that I was, and didn't recognise him at all until he said, 'I heard you talking about Bob Dylan'," said Chris. "Remember that this was after he had played here in 1996. He wanted to know what Bob was like and how he had been received in Liverpool. Then he asked if there was a place we could go for a drink. I said, 'well, you should know more about that than I do'."

But there had been some changes along the old street, where the girls used to sit on the fruit cartons as the beat groups walked by in their leathers. The Cavern they were now standing before wasn't the one George remembered. That was a few yards away under the rubble of a car park. This one was just a replica. Harrison explained all this and then said, "lead on".

The three of them – the Dylan enthusiast, the beautiful Mexican woman and one of the world's most famous men – walked together to the Crocodile pub in nearby Harrington Street.

"He was on Scotch and she was on orange juice because she was driving," said Chris, who was drinking bitter. They bought a round each, during which the talk spread over many subjects. "All the time I was thinking, someone is going to come along here – a heavy or something – and we'll be recognised. But they didn't. George had a big coat with a hat on and she did as well. He wasn't easy to recognise. The last time I had seen him was with Bob Dylan at the Wembley Arena in 1985."

Chris was asked if he had anything to do with the music business and was able to tell his companions that he was writing the biography of the folk singer Ralph McTell, later published as *The Streets of London*. "Ah yes, a good picker," said Harrison.

As he spoke about the meeting, Chris recalled a story that he had been told by his friend Dave Mattacks, the former drummer with Fairport Convention. On 9 December 1980, after the news of John Lennon's murder, Mattacks and some other musicians had been expected to do some recordings at Harrison's home, the 34-acre Friar Park in Henley-on-Thames. They all decided to cancel the session to show their respect for a fine musician and composer. But at lunchtime, said Chris, Mattacks received a telephone call from Harrison. 'Where the bloody hell is everyone?' he had asked. The drummer said that in the circumstances, they thought it should be called off. 'Don't be silly. No, I need to go on with it,' Harrison had said.

"That night, they all had dinner with Olivia in one of the big Gothic rooms with the stream running by it," said Chris. "Dave told me that George really opened up, came out with all these stories about the early Beatles. They all sat back looking at each other and they listened as George waxed lyrical about Lennon, speaking very fondly of him. He spoke very affectionately about John Lennon that night.

"On the day we met, he was very laid back," he said. "He had a cold. He had been visiting people up here and they had been to Ness Gardens (Liverpool University's botanical gardens, near Neston) because he is very much into horticulture. I bought them a drink. They bought me one. No one recognised them. It was just a chance thing. You see, oddly enough, I am not that interested in the Beatles. One of their fans would have been desperate to talk to him. But to me, he was a musician. Maybe for George that was the good thing. He wouldn't have wanted to meet an obsessive. He's a very nice man."

Yesterday, strangers from all over the world joined TV crews outside the Beatles Shop that Harrison had visited incognito all those years ago. Stephen Bailey became the shop's manager 17 years ago, three years after his life had been changed when he had heard Harrison's song, *Long Long Long* from the White Album. "It is such a beautiful song," he said. "George was a wonderful guy, so nice and peaceful and quiet. He's my favourite Beatle. He has done a lot of things that I believe in."

TRIBUTE TO BOB WOOLER

This article appeared on 19 February 2002 as a tribute to Bob Wooler, compere of The Cavern when the Beatles were begining.

~

His own taste was for the moody singers of the night – men like Frank Sinatra and women like Cleo Laine, who drew every emotion from the phrasing of a lyric, as they held the notes until smoke clouds from the cigarettes faded into the room's low lights. But Bob Wooler, who died early yesterday, aged 76, will be associated forever with the Beatles and the other Liverpool groups who appeared at The Cavern on Mathew Street, where he was the compere.

Of course, he knew the boys in the early days and they respected him as someone with a generous spirit and a keen wit, particularly when his tongue was fuelled by a tot or two. Yet, in the later years, when the Beatles' story had been blown into a legend, the cynical edge of his native city was heard from Bob in the bars. He had grown weary of hearing fanciful tales from strangers who had never met the Fab Four. For him, Mathew Street then became 'Myth-ew' Street.

Despite his prominence in the greatest story of rock 'n' roll, Bob was a man who lived aside from the mainstream. Towards the end of his life, he confided to Spencer Leigh, the authority on popular music, that his idea of hell was to be trapped in a room for days on end listening to someone fabricating stories about the Beatles. At the time, Spencer, whose shows *On The Beat* and *On The Merseybeat* are broadcast on Radio Merseyside, had been ghost-writing Bob's autobiography, a project that stalled before publication.

Writing and talking came easily to Bob. He delighted in word play of the sort used by John Lennon in his books *In His Own Write* and *A Spaniard In The Works*. Lennon, Bob said, had risen from "rage to riches". Brian Epstein was the 'Nemperor' (a reference to his music shops). These sayings were known as 'Woolerisms'. In the early 1960s, Bob wrote a column called, *Well Now, Dig This!* for *Mersey Beat*, the music paper edited by Bill Harry. In it, he prophesied great things for the Beatles.

Yesterday, tributes were coming in for the man who was raised in a gas-lit, two-up two-down house in Calthorpe Street, Garston, with his father, Tom, a dairy farmer who died at the age of 54, his mother, Florence, and younger brother, Jack. It was his years as a DJ at The Cavern, between 1961 and 1967, that people will remember, but Bob had been on the club scene before that, catching the end of the skiffle boom, while retaining his own enthusiasm for the music of an earlier era. Before his rock 'n' roll career, which began when he managed a group called the Kingstrums, Bob was a railway clerk. Then he did National Service, becoming a sergeant in the Army. Typically, he took his stripes off when he went home because his brother wouldn't have approved of his promotions.

He was secretive about his life, perhaps not wanting the groups to know that he was born in 1926, the year of the General Strike, making him 16 years older than the oldest Beatle, John Lennon. In the fashion of the moment, though, Bob brushed his hair forward and engaged in battles of wit with the younger men, as Liverpool humour swept the country in the wake of Beatlemania. There was not, however, a drop of Scouse in the accent of this compere who introduced the groups to the girls, dancing in their beehive hair-styles, black leather skirts and stockings with saucy seams. "Welcome to the best of cellars," he used to say, with vowels as rich as trifle. He would play a rock version of the *William Tell Overture* before the Beatles – whom he introduced at The Cavern about three hundred times – leapt on stage.

As a professional, he sometimes remonstrated with the performers for their sloppy diction and eccentric grammar, but they would just shrug their shoulders and smile. Bob believed in the Queen's English and his voice could have turned him into a national figure. He was meant to audition for Radio 1 in 1967, but failed to keep his appointment in circumstances never fully explained. Friends believe he simply wanted to stay in Liverpool, where he remained an influential man, though in the lean years of the 1970s he had to work in a hall as a bingo caller. "It was not my calling," he said afterwards, showing that his punning was as keen as ever. But he needed the money.

"Bob was exceptionally important to the music scene on Merseyside," said Spencer. "He was a very unusual man in so far as they were rough dance halls and they played raw rhythm 'n' blues music; the bouncers were tough, and yet he was a very cultured person indeed. He actually hated the Liverpool accent. His pet hate, in later years, were the three Bs – *Blackstuff, Bread* and *Brookside*. He thought those TV programmes gave a terrible impression of Liverpool."

Bill Harry said: "Bob was the man who advised the Beatles and all the other groups on their repertoire, their appearance on stage and their approach to the audience. He was a fine writer with a tremendous turn of phrase."

The days leading to his death at the Royal Liverpool Hospital, where he was being treated for a heart condition, were sad, but were lifted by the constant presence of his former wife, Beryl Adams, and messages from old friends, including Paul McCartney.

TRIBUTE TO LONNIE DONEGAN

I have always been wary of meeting my heroes – would my image of them be ruined by the reality? Dreams can be stronger than truth.

I came to know Lonnie Donegan, my boyhood hero, quite well towards the end of his life. I met him twice in person and we had several lengthy telephone conversations, all connected with articles I was writing about him. Lonnie had a reputation for being prickly with journalists, but that was not my experience.

He was driven directly from Manchester Airport to a café in Mathew Street, Liverpool, near The Cavern Club where he was to perform the following day. We had tea and biscuits and chatted for well over an hour.

Maybe he appreciated the fact that I knew quite a lot about him and his music – whatever the reason, we got on famously. He was absolutely charming. His reputation as a great influence on British music has continued to increase since his death. This article appeared on 5 November 2002, as a tribute to Lonnie.

~

When we were young, he was the biggest star in Britain. A small and dandy figure, with black hair swept back, he shook his head to the ever-quickening rhythm of a big acoustic guitar, strummed in imitation of the coming of a train from the distance.

Last night, we felt the last days of our childhood slipping away when the news broke that Lonnie Donegan was dead.

Those of us from that generation remembered how, as boys and girls in pullovers and jeans, we would leave the record store clutching a black record with the pink Pye colours circled around the hole. "Have you heard Lonnie's latest?" we would call to one another on the streets as we headed for the Dansette gramophones in the lounge at home. "Yes, it's great. Best yet."

Of course, Paul McCartney, John Lennon and George Harrison, were also among the schoolchildren expressing such sentiments. There were millions of us, some good singers, some bad, all enthusiasts. Lonnie was the spiritual 'daddy' of the Beatles and many other groups; the man who brought folk songs to suburban Britain from the swamps, the railroads, the hooded gambling dens, the brothels and the plantations of America.

He called his music 'skiffle', the name given to the house parties where poor people played their home-made instruments for friends and neighbours. As they picked out their tunes, drumming their feet and rocking to the rhythm, slugging whisky from a jar, someone would hand round a cap for donations to pay the rent.

In January 1956, Lonnie had his first big hit with *Rock Island Line*. Soon pale English boys were learning to play guitars and banjos. And the sounds of thimbled fingers rapping on washboards was heard in church halls and bedrooms across the land. Skiffle was the biggest teenage craze this country had ever known. Lonnie was its king.

An extraordinary string of hits was to follow in the next six years: *Cumberland Gap, Gambling Man* and *My Old Man's a Dustman* (all number ones), and *Battle of New Orleans, Michael Row the Boat Ashore, Pick a Bale of Cotton*. Many years later, Sir Paul McCartney was to say, "We studied his records avidly. We all bought guitars to be in a skiffle group. He was the man."

Unusually for a Briton, he was successful in the USA as well, reaching the American Top Ten with *Rock Island Line* and *Does Your Chewing Gum Lose Its Flavour On The Bedpost Overnight?* But, in 1962, the hits stopped, ironically just as the Beatles entered the charts for the first time with *Love Me Do*. The following years were not happy ones for Lonnie as he adjusted his essentially raw, folk/blues sound to the demands of TV and cabaret.

But the skiffle fans, now in the cardigans and slippers of late middle age, still hoped he would come back to them. In 2000, their wish was fulfilled when he joined Van Morrison to record an album, *Skiffle Sessions: Live In Belfast*. It was a success. "I have now achieved my final ambition to have one more hit. I wanted to give a massive raspberry to all those who thought I was washed up," he said. Later in the year, Lonnie was awarded the MBE. At the ceremony, Prince Charles said: "Not before time, Lonnie." Lonnie replied: "You're damn right, sir."

We all knew he had serious heart problems, eased by two major bypass operations, but he was back in demand, and nothing but the Almighty could stop him. So, in May last year, he accepted one of the greatest honours in his life when he was invited to appear at The Cavern in Liverpool. This meant that his name could be inscribed in the Wall of Fame, listing everyone who had performed there.

The day before that, he had walked Mathew Street like a tourist, wearing a huge woollen cardigan. There were a few puzzled stares, and then he was recognised. We had a cup of tea together in a local café. He was utterly charming, obviously proud of the skiffle legacy, still comparing it to the brasher rock and roll. "All roads lead to Lonnie really, because in the beginning was skiffle and the word was made rock," he said.

His performance, before more than four hundred people packed between the sweating walls, would have been terrific in a man of 20. He was 70. But when all the fast numbers were done, he ended by singing, *Irene Goodnight*. He called his audience "nice people" and waved as he left the stage. There was a maturity of tone in his voice few of us had heard before.

By then, his friends, like Carl Jones of Mold, with whom Lonnie stayed when he was in the North West, were urging him to slow down, but the little star would have none of it. "That wouldn't be Lonnie Donegan, would it?" he said.

In May this year, he underwent further heart surgery. A 25-date tour of the UK had already been arranged. Lonnie was immensely pleased that his 18-year-old son, Peter, a fine musician in his own right, was part of the act. They would have appeared together on Sunday at the Royal Court, Liverpool. "You know I'm calling this tour 'This Could Be The Last Time'," he had said.

"Do you think it will be?" I asked.

"Who knows?" he replied.

Last night, many of us had lumps in our throats. Goodbye Lonnie. Thanks for the songs that made our childhood.

SIR PAUL RETURNS TO THE CAVERN

On 14 December 1999, Sir Paul McCartney gave his fans a special treat for the Millennium by returning home to play at The Cavern Club for the first time in 36 years. The concert was based on Sir Paul's latest album, *Run Devil Run*, recorded as a tribute to the finest rock 'n' roll composers and performers of his generation.

~

Yes, it was throbbing again down the stairs of that fruity old cellar where the pouting girls with high skirts, beehive hair and a rare yearning, once met the thin boys leering in their leathers, in a union which was to change popular culture forever. And last night the greatest living rock 'n' roll star became the world's most

famous man as he ended the Millennium by returning to his native Liverpool to perform at The Cavern Club, home of so many dreams.

The girls, some now grannies, screamed again when Sir Paul McCartney slung the bass guitar over the shoulders of his black T-shirt and began singing *Hi-Ho Silver*. There he was, his eyebrows lifting and curling like baby caterpillars over that cherubic, oval-mouthed face, which, not so very long ago, had adorned the bedroom walls of almost every girl in the western world. With John Lennon, George Harrison, Pete Best, and later Ringo Starr, Sir Paul had been here 274 times before, refining his gift, that uncanny genius for melody, beneath the arched bricks.

Thirty-six years have gone by since the sweat last rinsed his brown head in the tiny cellar of sound. But there was no smell of onions, no hot dog buns bleeding their tomato ketchup this time. Instead, there were pressmen and women, and the cables, lights and paraphernalia of the technological age, paying homage to a boy from Liverpool.

Once he entertained dozens at fairgrounds and church halls, and counted his luck. Last night's concert is expected to be shown to a global audience of 600 million, including those tuning into the Internet. Life is strange.

"It's been a long time coming, but its good to be back," Sir Paul yelled to the heaving throng, and the guitars started wailing to *Hi Ho Silver*.

With him, was his "brave band of minstrels" – Mick Green (guitar), formerly of Johnny Kidd and the Pirates, Dave Gilmour (guitar) of Pink Floyd, keyboard player Pete Wingfield and Ian Paice (drums) of Deep Purple. It was a concert of consummate professionalism, touched by moments of poignancy and celebration as the band filled just 50 minutes with 13 songs.

With a shrug of his shoulders, Sir Paul launched into the Buddy Holly classic,

Brown Eyed Handsome Man. Who on Earth could he have been thinking of?

"It's going to warm up – don't worry," he said, as the steam began rising.

References were made to his love of Liverpool. But he was speaking with real feeling, garnished with sarcasm, when he said, "It's good here, isn't it? The Cavern is up there somewhere under the rubble – another brilliant city council decision. Hey! Let's bury The Cavern!" The original cellar is actually a few yards away under the car park where the immense media tribe gathered to report the event to the world. But the new club mirrors the old one almost exactly.

There were the songs of sorrow: *Lonesome Town, Place of Broken Dreams, Where the Streets are Filled with Regret*. And then he opened *I Don't Want No Other Baby*, his voice hoarse and sore with emotion. No words were spoken, but there can be no doubt that Linda was back with him in those moments. Sadness filled the cherub eyes. The stage glowed pink, purple and green. "No other baby could thrill me like you do." There was stillness now. They were singing into the great highways of loneliness, and everyone knew it.

Someone asked for the Rolling Stones' *Satisfaction*. "There is a little wag in the crowd," said Sir Paul to cheers. "Look at my lips," he added impishly. Rock 'n' roll moods move fast!

Paul called on the audience to applaud Bob Wooler, former Cavern DJ. "He's here, the guy who used to introduce us from the side."

A bottle blonde, glamorous in tight black leather trousers, studded belt, and short sleeves, was dancing like they used to. It was All Shook Up – yeah, like a volcano that's hot. With the opening bars of, *I Saw Her Standing There*, the hall was jumping, even the middle-aged journalists with beer in their bellies and deadlines on their minds. *Let's Have a Party* ended the set in fine rocking style. Paul McCartney was home, the proud son, welcomed again by his people. "Thank you, goodbye, see you next time," he shouted with a wave. The many calls for an encore were not answered.

Earlier, at a press conference, Sir Paul said: "I love Liverpool and there is no better way to rock out the century. This is where it all began and this is where the century ends. It is rock 'n' roll and The Beatles – a great little rock band."

As the television lights shone brightly on the stage Sir Paul blinked, moving his head from side-to-side, before giving the cameras his trademark, two-thumbed salute. "There is no more fantastic place to rock out the century. Thank you very much for coming. God bless you all."

His publicist and friend Geoff Baker said: "This is one of the wildest nights of his career and he has had a good few wild nights." With a smile, he added: "It's a shame, a shame that the one person in the world who is not going to see Paul McCartney is Paul McCartney."

Another missing face, of course, belonged, but Geoff Baker said that his co-writer was always there in their hearts and thoughts. Sadness combined with exhilaration as the crowds departed last night.

Alan Williams, the Beatles' first manager, was sitting in the de Coubertins sports bar remembering "his boys", in the free flow of his red wine. "He still owes me fifteen quid, you know," he said, but some people have heard that story before. It's always good for a reunion when you kiss the good faces of old friends and offer your hand to hazy strangers. The concert was being relayed on 13 screens in the bar, but Alan, the man who sold the Beatles, may not have noticed too much.

Alex McKechnie, 55, The Cavern's promoter, was looking terrific in his winkle-pickers, trousers pressed to a razor edge, and Beatles jacket. His normal crew-cut had been grown into a Beatle fringe just for the occasion. For him, this was not just a night. It was history. The opinion was shared by his younger colleagues Alan Roberts, 22, the stage manager, and Dave Catterall, 20, the house engineer.

"Whenever the talk is of guitar groups, people think first of the Beatles," said Dave.

Housewife Kathy Noonan, 51, had been there first time round. "It was brilliant. I was just over the moon to be back in The Cavern. I used to stop off school and sit outside the old Cavern on the fruit cartons listening to them playing."

Up the street, in Battys bar, *Twist and Shout* was shaking the walls, where the faithful waited. But this was not the Beatles. The group was called the Blue Meanies. And they looked as young as the boys on the photos on the old bedroom walls. Their sound, though, was a tribute to something precious that is forever Liverpool.

THE LEGENDARY DIXIE DEAN

2001 saw the unveiling of a statue to remember the record-breaking hero, Dixie Dean. This article is based on interviews with people who knew and loved him.

He came to stand in front of the big man's statue, just like thousands of other tourists and fans, but for John Keith, the moment held added poignancy, for he was one of the last people to see the living smile on the face of Dixie Dean. The memory is with him now as he stares, almost ten feet up, at the bronze muscles of a neck which gave Dixie's head a thrusting power never equalled before or since on the football field.

~

It was 1 March 1980, derby day. Three men were travelling up Scotland Road towards Goodison Park in the back seat of a black cab. John Keith was in the middle, turning his head like a spectator at a ping-pong match, as the other two pitched words at each other. On one side was Bill Shankly, the manager whose flinty wit and resolute spirit came to symbolise Liverpool's rise to the top of European football. On the other was Dixie Dean of Everton and England, quite simply the best centre-forward ever. The words John heard were of affection and

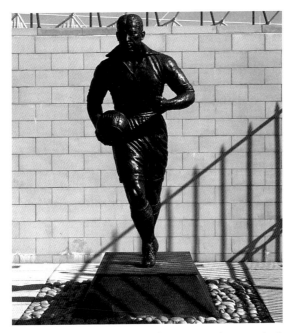

respect exchanged between two men who had found fame with their passion for kicking and heading a ball of stitched leather.

Less than three hours later, William Ralph (Dixie) Dean was dead. He had suffered a heart attack shortly after the match during which Everton's Peter Eastoe scored in the 73rd minute to cut Liverpool's lead to 2-1.

Earlier, Bill and Dixie had been at a lunch to launch the Everton and Liverpool annuals produced by photographer Harry Ormesher and John Keith, who was then in the middle of his 30-year spell as a football reporter with the *Daily Express*. During the speeches, Bill had eulogised about Dixie, who, by arrangement with the publisher, was to be John's special guest at the match. They had left for Goodison in the taxi. Then John took up his seat in the *Express* box and Dixie joined the other guests and VIPs in the directors' box.

After the match, Bill met John. "Did you make a note of what I was saying about him at the lunch?" he asked. "That's his obituary."

Dixie's ashes were spread on the centre line of the turf where he had led Everton to so many victories.

I ask John, author of *Dixie Dean: The Inside Story of a Football Icon*, why he thinks that Dixie is the one representative from that generation whose name is heard as often now as it was then. After all, hundreds of great footballers have come and gone, and they are now almost forgotten except by the game's statisticians. But all the fans, whatever their age, in the Gwladys Street stand, know about Dixie. Sometimes, on grey afternoons, they wish he would return to Goodison Park with his mighty chest swelling a blue shirt.

"My father saw him play and people of that generation are still in awe," says John. "When you mention his name, there is a resonance of greatness that I don't think is engendered by anyone else I have ever heard about."

John has been a journalist on Merseyside since 1966, the year England won the World Cup, Everton won the FA Cup and Liverpool were League Champions. Now he concentrates on match analysis, broadcasting (including Radio Merseyside's popular fans' phone-in on Saturday evenings) and writing books. He has written biographies about Bill Shankly and Bob Paisley.

"This man symbolises English football," says John. "You can see it all in the statue; the laces on the ball, the old-fashioned boots, the parting down the middle of his hair. Dean's story has been handed down from grandfather, to father, to son, even mother to daughter. He was a favourite with the women because he was a very good-looking guy.

"There's a story about him being in London when Pathé News came to do a piece about him. The make-up man came over with some powder. 'I'm just going to take the shine off your face, Mr Dean,' he said. 'If you come near me with that, I'll take the shine off your face,' replied the supremely fit centre-forward of almost twelve stone, rising to his full height of five foot ten inches. But his greatest strength was in his neck. He used to practise heading with a medicine ball stuffed with paper, which must have weighed a rock. Even the old leather footballs must have seemed like a balloon compared to a medicine ball."

Although the rewards in the game were comparatively modest in his day, Dixie was one of the first players to receive mass adulation. After his playing days, Dixie's life was less successful. He didn't have the financial cushion of management, media contracts, and personal appearances that keep today's players in fine style. For a while, he ran the Dublin Packet pub in Chester and then he was given a job at Littlewoods by John Moores, then owner of Everton.

In 1964, they held a testimonial match for him at Goodison, which raised £9,000.

"But Michael Owen probably earns more in a week than Dixie earned in his whole life," says John with a rueful smile. "But he was never a jealous man. He didn't envy the modern players."

In 1976, in a cruel twist of fate, Dixie's right leg had to be amputated. His slow recovery required courage of a different sort, but Dixie rose to this challenge.

Four years later came the taxi ride. "I asked Dixie Dean when he had last watched a derby match," recalls John. "Amazingly, he told us that, at his last one, he was a player."

The statue of Dixie was commissioned by Everton from the sculptor Tom Murphy, who has also created statues of Bill Shankley, John and Cecil Moores, Johnny Walker RN and John Lennon. The complicated casting work was done by foundryman Chris Butler. It was unveiled by Bill Kenwright, Everton's vice chairman, on the 73rd anniversary of that sunny spring afternoon when Dixie scored his 60th League goal of the season. At the unveiling, fans recalled the moment when the wee Scottish winger, Alec Troup, lofted the ball from the corner flag. 'Their Dixie' rose until he hovered high above all other players. Then, with a single thrust of his piston-power neck, he headed the ball past the Arsenal goalkeeper and into football history. Sixty thousand men, women and children roared in a way never heard before or since in the famous old ground. For more than eight minutes they saluted this hero, the son of a train driver from the north end of Birkenhead who had broadened his shoulders lifting crates on a milk round.

Dixie was at Everton until 1938, scoring 377 goals in 431 League and FA Cup games. In 1927/28, when Dixie secured his record, Everton won the First Division championship. Prior to joining Everton, Dixie had been at Tranmere Rovers where he scored 27 goals in 27 games.

The ceremony for the unveiling of the statue was attended by a huge crowd of fans and also by Dixie's daughter, Barbara Dean with her daughter Melanie Prentice and grandchildren Daniel Dean and Scarlet Rose, and Dixie's sons William and Godfrey.

Bill Kenwright said, "The word legend is over-used in a game where the pay packet and egos rule. There is a little of the hero in some people who wear the shirt up and down the country, though not all of them by any means. But today we salute probably the greatest hero of all time. Our beloved William Ralph (Dixie) Dean has made us all proud to be Evertonians."

For Geoffrey Dean, it was simpler than that: "He was as good a father as he was a footballer."

EARNIE SHAVERS GOES THE DISTANCE

The great Muhammad Ali once said of Earnie Shavers, "Earnie hit me so hard, he shook my kinfolk back in Africa." This article was written in February 1999 and records an interview in which Earnie reflects on his early years in the American Deep South and the day he let Muhammad Ali get away.

~

Earnie Shavers was just five years old when the Ku Klux Klan visited the family's humble farm. His father had failed to keep up the payments on a mule. Some weeks earlier, Curtis Shavers had bought the scrawny pack beast to help ease the load on his 20-acre spread. The deal had been clinched deep in the American South where, in the dark of night, crazy men still carried fiery crosses and wore pointed hoods over their heads, with slits for the eyes.

Times were tough for Curtis and his wife Willie Belle and their ten children, growing wheat, corn and oats on the tired soil of Alabama, so Curtis fell behind with his payments. Not a wise move for a black man scratching dirt for a living in the little town of Garland, where segregation of the races was the strict rule from the cradle to the grave. To make matters worse, the white mule seller turned out to be a Klansman.

Drizzle brushes greyly against the windows of Mason's Café, on Hoylake Road in Moreton, where Earnie tells his story, far from the heat of the Deep South.

"My father had this mule that he had bought off some white fellow and he didn't pay him like he should. He paid some of it but he didn't pay it all because he was trying to make ends meet. The guy came by to take the mule back. They were in the yard and the man said, 'I have come to take the mule away' and my father said 'no'. My father pulled a gun on him. The guy was a Klansman. There is a moral to this story: if you were living in Alabama in the fifties, you don't pull a gun on a Klansman."

The pitch of Earnie's voice rises in synchrony with his hand gestures as he canters across the memories triggered by the word 'Klansman'. Then he laughs. The sound makes you think of treacle melting over a sponge. At the time, it wasn't so funny. That night, the Klansmen came a-calling with their flour-bag-hats and their torches. They were surrounding the house.

"We thought, 'Oh my God, here they come!' They were saying: 'We know he's in there. We know the nigger is in there'."

But, unbeknown to the Klan, Curtis wasn't there. "My grandfather had got him on a train, heading north," says Earnie. Exactly what had forewarned the old man of danger wasn't clear, but you had to be smart in the South in those days.

Curtis found a job making car bumpers in a factory near Youngstown, Ohio, and six months later the rest of the family joined him. At the local high school, Earnie excelled at American football. The potential of this muscular six footer as an all-round athlete was obvious.

In 1967, when Earnie was 22 and had two children by his childhood sweetheart and wife, La Verne, he was introduced to the boxing trainer, Pedro Tomez, in a local gym. At the time he was working in a car factory which he hated because he felt "caged". Walking through the door, Tomez said: "Boy, with a build like that, you'll be champion of the world some day". His words were to prove just a few dazed seconds short of this prophecy.

Earnie, his trademark shaven head shining like varnished teak, was clutching a mug of coffee in his huge hands while his girlfriend Sue Clegg listened to him talk of racism in America. Earnie settled in Moreton in 1997. He also acts as an adviser to her nephew, the professional light heavyweight Kenny Rainford. It seemed strange, but the man of whom the great Muhammad Ali once said, "Earnie hit me so hard, he shook my kinfolk back in Africa", didn't seem at all bitter.

Did the Klansmen injure him or his mother? "Oh, no. The Klan, you know, they had some honour, they didn't bother with kids or women, these ones didn't anyway, no problem. They looked for him and he was gone. It was the best move that happened to us. We got north and my whole life changed. I got to do some different things and the fighting was one of them. It was so much better."

The forgiveness in the heart of this man, later to be feared for the hardest punch in boxing, stretches back to the God-fearing ways of his Baptist mother. Even the visit of the Klan and the insults which black people accepted as routine in the segregated South, didn't sow in him a hatred of whites.

"My mother instilled that in us. She kept hammering over and over and over that we all belong to God. We are all God's children, black or white. Some are good and some are bad. All my family have done well because of my mother. She always taught us to love everyone. 'God, he loves us all', she would say. That's how we all made it, on my mother's prayers. God opened his door to us all."

It is a philosophy that Earnie has passed on to his own children, Tammy, Cynthia, Catherine, Carla, Katherine, Amy, Natasha, Lisa and Earnie (Junior).

"I have a lot of white friends and a lot of black friends," says Earnie. "One day, my oldest daughter Tammy said, 'Daddy, Daddy, Daddy, one of your white friends came by.' I said, 'Tammy, sit down. Daddy has white friends and Daddy has black friends and all of Daddy's friends got names. Tammy, I never want to hear you say that one of Daddy's white friends came by. If you can't remember the name, say one of your friends came by.' She said, 'Daddy, I never heard you say that when one of your black friends came by'."

Willie Belle lived to see her son rise up the heavyweight rankings, watching both his amateur and professional bouts.

"She would be fighting harder than me, shouting 'Leave him alone!'" His voice soars to a falsetto here. Sometimes Earnie feared that she might have a heart attack, or rush into the ring with her shoe off to give his opponent the benefit of her accomplished backhand and definite opinions.

It was a glorious career, peaking in the 1970s, now known as 'the golden era of heavyweights'. His opponents included Jimmy Ellis, Jerry Quarry, Ron Lyle, Ken Norton, Joe Bugner, Jimmy Young and Randy 'Tex' Cobb. He had two world title shots, most famously in 1977 when he "stunned" Ali several times during the 15 rounds, which he lost narrowly on points.

Two years later, he floored Larry Holmes. "For seven seconds, I was champion of the world," recalled Earnie. Unhappily, Holmes regained his feet to take the fight in the 11th round.

In his career, Earnie won 82 fights, lost 15 and drew one, but it was his epic struggle with Ali that gained him a permanent place in the history of boxing.

"He's a very nice guy, one of my best friends," says Earnie. "It was about four years prior to fighting him that we became friends. He invited me up to his training camp where he would tell me how to fight the fighters he knew about. He had a lot of speed for a big guy.

"Ali didn't have the greatest punch but he had a lot of speed. He moved all the time. He was hard to catch and punch, but in our fight I did catch him a few times. I hurt him. He was out in the second round. I was programmed to go the distance, but you don't beat Ali going the distance. He told me that if I had followed up in the second I would have knocked him out, 'But you let me get away', he said. Ali just took a split second to recuperate. I thought he was faking the hurt. He was cunning. If I had followed up, I would have been world champion.

"But it wasn't meant to be. God had other plans for me. The Ali fight opened every door in and out of the ring. I have had opportunities I never dreamed of before. It was a great honour for me to fight him, even though I didn't win. My heart says you want to win and you don't want to win, but I let him off the hook." Ali received $3m dollars and Earnie just $300,000.

As he speaks, Earnie, who is 54 and weighs 230lb, just five pounds above his prime weight, occasionally emphasises a point by thumping his right fist into his left palm. Just one of those punches would be enough to guarantee you a fat invalidity pension for the rest of your days. But you might not think it worth the risk. As the table ceased trembling, he smiled at his girlfriend, Sue. The shoppers walked by the steamed windows, unaware that sitting inside was the man with the biggest punch in the world.

Earnie and Sue start to banter. "If I lost all my money, would you still love me?" he asks. "Earnie, I could never stop loving you, but I sure would miss you," he answers himself with another rumbling laugh.

"There are a thousand small things that make a fighter," he says. "That's why very few people make it, because they don't want to do the thousand small things. Don't drink, don't do drugs, leave the girls alone. You have to do the same thing whether you have the talent or not … no gunslinger, babe."

A BIRTHDAY DOWN THE JAM BUTTY MINES

An affectionate piece written for 8 February 2002, the birthday of Liverpool's much-loved Ken Dodd,who came top in a poll by the *Liverpool Echo* and Radio Merseyside to find the 100 Great Merseysiders in April 2003.

~

It's a great moment in show business history. People across the land should be raising glasses of champagne to Ken Dodd, in thanks and celebration of the comic genius, hailed by millions as the funniest in Britain. For the *Daily Post* can reveal that the coal merchant's son from Knotty Ash is 75 today. The trouble is that the man himself may not know that he has reached this dizzy perch in his fine career.

You see, in *Who's Who*, which invites the famous to send in their own entries, his date of birth is listed as 8 November 1931, making him 71. *Chambers Biographical Dictionary* prefers 1929, as does the *Cambridge Biographical Encyclopaedia*. However, in his compilation of Mersey Stars, published in 2000, the Reverend Michael Smout, Canon of Aughton Parish Church, placed the date as 8 November 1927. If you look at Ken's birth certificate, you can see that was right.

Of course, when you have been blessed with hair like a bird's nest styled in a storm, teeth like a toboggan run and the soaring pitch of a sentimental balladeer, numbers are a trifling concern.

As the late George Carman QC observed during the 1989 trial, when Ken was cleared of tax offences, "Some accountants are comedians but comedians are never accountants."

Ken, whose feather-duster fashioned into a tickling stick is as much a national symbol as Britannia's trident, is the great survivor of the old Variety Stage. At the age of eight he was presenting Punch and Judy shows at his primary school, advancing into the ventriloquist act that he performed one Christmas Day at St Edward's Orphanage, Knotty Ash.

Although known in the area for his coal deliveries, Arthur Dodd, Ken's father, gave his occupation as musician-saxophonist (theatre orchestra) on the birth certificate. Indeed, he had played in the Knotty Ash village hall and was a professional musician for a while in the 1920s. On leaving the local Holt High School at 14, Ken joined the family business, while reading extensively in the library, particularly favouring the works of Mark Twain and PG Wodehouse. Meanwhile, he had branched out by selling bleach, firelighters and home-made soap, tested by his mother, Sarah. During this time, Ken developed his true talent as Professor Chuckbutty and other crazy characters.

The big break came on 27 September 1954 at the Nottingham Empire when he was a small name on the bill. "Not as big as the printer's," he recalled ruefully. From there he went to Leeds, Sunderland, and the House of Terror (the Glasgow Empire), affectionately known as the comedian's graveyard on account of its reputation for making and breaking careers.

By the end of the 1950s, Ken was making regular appearances on TV as well as in the country's best theatres. Hit records followed, including *Love is like a Violin*

36

and *Happiness and Tears*, securing his place as the country's top all-round entertainer.

"I love comedy," said the self-styled Squire of Knotty Ash. You never stop learning. Comedy is wonderful." Bob Monkhouse, Eric Sykes, Jimmy Tarbuck and Roy Hudd are among his admirers, but his most important fans will always be sitting in the flip-back seats of our theatres, the old matrons chortling away in their surgical-support stockings, their men dreaming of the high-kicking girls in fishnet tights and the little boys and girls with candy-floss encrusted hair.

Stephen Shakeshaft, the *Daily Post's* picture editor, has followed the career of the man who has made him ache with laughter. "I remember having a cup of tea with Harry, the stage-door man at the Royal Court, Liverpool," he said. "It was six minutes before curtains up on the first house. But Harry said there was nothing to worry about. And, sure enough, the door opens and a pile of leaves blows in, followed by Ken in his trilby hat, overcoat and scarf. You wouldn't think this was the man who was going to entertain over a thousand people. Doddy asks me into his dressing-room, takes off his overcoat, puts on his red 'moggy' coat and rubs make-up on his face. He says, 'I'll be back in a minute, help yourself to a lager.' I sat there listening to his act on a little speaker. Then he walked back in the room, I took the picture and we continued our conversation. He has a lovely face, a very caring face."

Happy birthday, Ken, and many more of 'em.

HARD TIMES

SCOTLAND ROAD

From a distance, there is a certain romance in poverty. When you are there, it's different. The new generation wrote songs about what the old generation suffered. But it is important that we should never forget how it was – for some. Our writing is all we have left to offer.

~

These articles were written between July and August 2002 in advance of the 200th anniversary of Scotland Road's development into the houses, pub and churches that are famous around the world.

SOME SERIOUS QUAFFING

There were ways of telling the neighbours you were doing fine, even when you could orchestrate the rumbles in the tummies of your children as they sat, whey-faced, in a row in the parlour, where visions of the little coffin in the corner were still raw in the memory. But the man of the house sat on his doorstep, sharpening a knife on the stone, waiting for the good people to scurry home from the Christmas morning Mass with their cheeks flushed by the cold of the wind sweeping in from the river.

"By Jaisus," they said, "now that family must have a rare bird roasting inside for their man to need such a keen blade."

But their man was hungry, scraping his knife and salivating over the smells in his imagination, though his eyes were still red-webbed with the drinks he had raised the night before. One after another they were downed in exuberant succession, to quell the shame he felt about the empty table at home. Maybe enough money could always be found for drink, but it stretched to precious little else. So, with a little performance on the doorstep, you could fool the neighbours into thinking the family inside was gathering for a grand feast.

To the stranger, it is difficult to feel the truth about Scotland Road, the track that for generations was regarded as the pulse of old Liverpool. This is the road that reputedly had a pub on every corner, though some particularly thirsty blocks had one in the middle as well. It is the address that people from all over the world associate with Liverpool, along with Lime Street and Mathew Street.

On one side, you have the romance of poverty, told in voices stewed in folklore and heard in sentimental songs before the barmaid with the plump biceps hangs the white towels on the taps. On the other side is the anger and the bitterness, which dwells just a light rub beneath the surface. Mostly, the two seem to be joined in a flow of stories from Scotland Road and the streets just off it.

This was the greatest concentration of Irish people to be found anywhere outside Dublin and Cork. Yet Scotland Road was host to people of many races – the Italians with their fast fists and plaster figures of Mary and Jesus on the mantel, the Jewish tailors, the Welsh slate-chippers and builders whose strict manners were cut in chapels on distant hills, the Germans and their sausages and songs, the Norse sailors who had seen many lands.

Again, there were contradictions. The Italians may have been boxers, fish-fryers and ice cream-scoopers, but they also laid mosaic and terrazzo in exquisite patterns and rolled melodies from barrel-organs; the Irish were fond of a drink, but they also loved stories and poetry, giving the Liverpool accent a lyrical lilt that can still be heard in some comedians; and the Welsh were poets and singers too, and their vision of a higher life can be seen in buildings all over Merseyside.

The popular image of Scotland Road as 'little Ireland' grew after the potato famine of the 1840s when countless starving people crossed the water to Liverpool, but the Irish population in the port had been quite large before that. The first big influx followed the rebellion at the end of the eighteenth century, which resulted in General Gerard Lake's bloody English victory at the Battle of Vinegar Hill in 1798. As atrocity and counter-atrocity followed each other, thousands fled the country.

In an earlier age, however, the stretch now known as Scotland Road, had been of geographical significance. In the 1330s, a white cross had been laid as a marker at a spot near the present Hopwood Street. A well-worn track ran from there and, in a map of 1821, the site was described as 'the remains of the ancient cross'. Fifty years before that, the track had been widened into a turnpike road. It went north through Walton, Burscough, Preston, Lancaster and up to Scotland. Gracious people sauntered over the grass, before eating Kitty Eccleston's meat pies. A further widening in 1803 brought custom to the area. Houses, shops, pubs and businesses were established along its course. This was the true beginning of the famous Scotland Road, which ran the 1,640 yards from Scotland Place to Boundary Street.

Now, a few descendants of the old families have gathered about a mile away in the Seel Street gallery of Tony Brown, an artist, who is working on designs of posters, mugs and T-shirts to celebrate next year's 200th anniversary of Scotland Road. He wants his designs to be simple and colourful. Soon the conversation is crackling. This is not history as it would be recorded in books, but you begin to understand how this road came to symbolise a city of high emotion, where the people could take the blows but felt the pain very deeply. It was a pain that lasted, and it could be seen in the faces on family photographs on the sideboard.

The songs and newspapers told of a spirit that could overcome adversity. Maybe. We are talking about disease, atrocious housing and sanitary conditions, child mortality, cruel working conditions, unemployment and hunger. From this emerged the strong woman, the indomitable mother. To the Catholic Church, they were the successors of Mary, bearing their grief and their trials with a stalwart countenance. All the men speak with great affection of the women who kept the families together. They were there when the Luftwaffe dropped its bombs and when the great strikes stilled the cranes along the waterfront. It was mother's hand that stuffed the Christmas stocking with apples, oranges and little toys, and laid it on the end of the bed where the children slept. People speak lightly of miracles, but this came close to the real thing.

When speaking of Scottie Road, people include the numerous small streets that ran off it, adding their own peculiarities to the wider picture. Although many of the street names survive, the community was broken up by post-war clearance programmes and developments. The new properties have amenities beyond the dreams of the old residents, but the area remains poor, with all the usual social problems that spread like bindweed when the community spirit dies. Even so, you can spot an old Scottie Roader by his walk – a kind of cock-of-the-parade strut, born in hope and sustained by arrogance, not unlike that of a gun-slinger entering the saloon of a frontier town. At the beginning of the last century, he could have chosen from 246 pubs on Scotland Road and its immediate vicinity, serving the congregations of 14 Catholic churches.

"That is many more than a large town would have had," says the 65-year-old chairman of the local Vauxhall History and Heritage Group, Terry Cooke, who wrote *Scotland Road: The Old Community* and *The Pubs of Scotland Road*. In the 1950s there were still 158 pubs. Now just four remain – the Parrot, the Eagle, the Throstles Nest and the Hamlet.

"Look at the tragedies that befell the people of Scotland Road from the early nineteen hundreds – the First World War, when so many signed up and didn't come back, and the strikes," says Terry.

Billy Woods, a 69-year-old retired painter and decorator, says that people from villages all over Lancashire came, hoping to sail to the New World. "But when they got here, many of them didn't have the fares to go further, others fell ill, some decided to stay. They married here and the community grew," he adds. "People say to me 'We can tell you're from Scotland Road by the way you walk with a swagger'."

Billy's parents – seafarer Ted and his wife Jean – were from the area. They had seven children.

"One of the reasons I am against the establishment is that I look around me and I see all these fine buildings and I hear how these people get praised – you know, they left this and that to the city. But I look and I think, where did they get the money from? I'll tell you. They got it from my grandfather, his father and his father, who lived in abject poverty. The kids today ask why they didn't do anything about their poverty. But they had to put a crust on the table, pay the rent and do all these things. If they said 'boo' to the boss they were up the road, no messing. You went there and then.

41

"If you had no money you had to go to the Parish (Poor Law funds), which was the most humiliating experience. You practically had to get down on your hands and knees to get any money. We are classified as arrogant and militant, but it comes from those days. We're very forceful when we talk and we talk very fast, so that we can get in what we're going to say before someone stops us. We came from people who had it bad. They paid the price for what we have got now."

Yet there were good times. He recalls how you could get a pocketful of brown sugar from the Tate and Lyle refinery. The woman next door to his grandma would heat it on a pan with bicarbonate of soda to make jumbo toffee.

"The women were brilliant," says Billy. "The saying was 'keep her pregnant and keep her happy'. But it was really keep her pregnant and short of money."

"If they couldn't afford anything else, at least they could give you love, affection and protection," says Terry. "They could give you a happy Christmas from almost nothing."

Also chatting in the group were Mike Kelly, a 70-year-old local historian, 54-year-old Freddy O'Connor, author of *Liverpool: Our City - Our Heritage* and *A Pub On Every Corner*, and 82-year-old Jim Fitzsimons, a retired printer. The stories roll amid gusts of laughter.

Jim was raised in the area with his seven brothers and sisters and he has a good line in patter about the three-day wakes they held in those days. At one, the Irish labourers came in to pay their respects to an 'auld divil'. After some serious quaffing, everyone began dancing. Such was their enthusiasm that the floor gave way, depositing the entire funeral party, body and all, in the cellar.

THE FAMINE

You can talk of the romance of it all – the patched glamour of people pleased to tell you that the bobbies had to walk in pairs for their own protection, the kids dribbling cans in the jiggers behind the houses, the shawled Mary Ellens carrying baskets of fruit on their heads, the devout swots hoping for a place in a seminary, the pubs where toothless crones rattled their spoons to the rhythm of a squeeze-box, and then there were those priests striding the beat like crows in their black, to accept tea and biscuits in the homes of the poor and faithful parishioners – it's all true. But one event overwhelmed everything else: the Irish Potato Famine.

Those words still spread a cold web over the feelings of descendants from the old community. Sometimes, you have to measure words and their meaning, instead of just glossing over them as you advance to the next paragraph.

Consider this. In the bad years, more than 80 per cent of children born in Scotland Road and the streets immediately off it died before they were ten. The poor, haggard women, who spent so much of their lives pregnant to give their men

a few moments of pleasure in fetid cellars, were delivering babies for the undertaker. In fact, the priests were present at the births to baptise the babies, so that they would enter Heaven.

Central to all this was St Anthony's Church, which celebrates its bi-centenary in 2004. In the early days, it would have served a moderately prosperous Catholic congregation of business people and farmers, but it was to become the church most associated with the Famine.

In 1847, 116,000 Irish refugees arrived at the Clarence Steamship dock, mostly from the Gaelic-speaking west. Many carried the seeds of typhus in their bodies. During the year, 60,000 of them were treated for the disease and another 40,000 for dysentery and diarrhoea.

There is some uncertainty about the final death count. However, we do know that 2,303 men, woman and children were buried in St Anthony's ground that year. A few richer ones were entombed in the crypt, where they charged one and a half guineas (about £1.60) for a berth, but there wasn't enough room for all the bodies, particularly those passing daily from the workhouse on Brownlow Hill.

In the same year, 7,219 paupers were found mass graves at St Mary's churchyard, Cambridge Street, near the site of the old Myrtle Street Children's Hospital. When this was full, the bodies were taken to St Martin-in-the-Field in Oxford Road, off Vauxhall Road.

Among the dead in that dreadful year were ten priests, known as the Martyrs of the Famine. The priests knelt or rested on their haunches beside the rags of the dying, to rub their holy oil, infirmarium, on to the eyelids, the ears, the mouths, the hands, and finally the foreheads of those ones who waited. And the lice which spread the fever, crawled into the clothing of the priests and the doctors, and the men who tended the souls and bodies of the sick became, themselves, carriers of death. Their housekeepers, too, were victims, as they handled their coats.

Well, it was all a long time ago. But Father Tom Williams, the 54-year-old priest at St Anthony's for the past 13 years, speaks of it with rare passion. The Scotland Road he knew as a child grew from this legacy.

Tom and his sisters, Margaret and Marie, and brother, Richard, were brought up in a ground floor dwelling in Ashfield Gardens, attending Ashfield Road Primary School. Their parents were Richard, a bargee on the Leeds/Liverpool Canal, and Margaret, a cleaner. Like many of his generation, Tom was drawn to the priesthood and began boarding at the Christleton Hall seminary, Chester, when he was 13. With his early ambition to be a right-half on the football field dashed by his tendency to toe-poke the ball, Father Williams went to St Sylvester's secondary school before studying for the priesthood at the theological college in Lisbon, Portugal.

Now he is sitting in the comfortable lounge of the priest's house at St Anthony's, which just edges ahead of its next-door neighbour, the Throstles Nest pub, to be the most distinguished building in the area. Both have large and loyal congregations.

"Liverpool, particularly this area, is really a hotch-potch," he says. "People think of the potato famine, but Irish people had been coming here in quite large numbers before that. With the diseases and poor sanitation, conditions around here were abysmal. The infant mortality was phenomenal. From our records, we can say that, of all those baptised, forty-seven per cent were dead within a week and eighty-six per cent died before they were ten. They said that the men of Scotland Road weren't good enough to join the Army because of the state of their teeth and their brittle bones. "They weren't even good enough to be cannon fodder," adds the priest, and you can tell that this is a man who sticks up for his people. But those brittle bones saw some action on the fields of France during the First World War. Many are still there.

Gradually, life improved, though Scotland Road remained one of the most deprived areas of Liverpool, with more than 100,000 people packed into the area, reaching an estimated peak of 150,000 in the 1860s.

A little surprisingly, Father Williams readily admits that the popular image of standing-room only in the churches is seen through a rosy haze.

"I know priests who were here in the nineteen thirties who say that men going to church was never a strong point on Scotland Road. Actually, I think the faith is strong now. You have only got to see the response to baptisms and funerals and the sense of respect. Going to Mass on a Sunday is a different matter. There has always been a strong sense of parish. This was because of the schools that the children attended between five and fourteen. The football teams encouraged a great sense of rivalry between the parish schools. I remember going to Goodison Park in the fifties to see Saint Sylvester's play Saint Anthony's and there must have been thirteen thousand in the crowd."

But there is something that puzzles outsiders. Why did Scotland Road become so famous? After all, there were lots of poor districts in Liverpool.

"It was very busy," replies Father Williams. "We were close to the docks. The seamen who travelled the world identified with Scotland Road. There were the riots against the police in nineteen eleven. The Rotunda was a popular music-hall and the trams and buses ran up and down. Because the pubs were on Scotland Road, it was the social centre. All the other places seemed like tributaries.

"But there was a sense of snobbery in other parts of the city – from those in Anfield and Kensington. You know, 'You're not from Scotland Road, are you?' I remember the 'johnnies', as we used to call them, walking in a straight line with the washing on their heads on their way to the wash-house. These were Africans from the boats. But it wasn't a derogatory term, there was nothing like that. They looked so odd in their bright orange shirts and brown suits," smiles Father Williams.

Scotland Roaders were accustomed to mixing with people of different races, so prejudice really had no place. In their blunt acceptance of strangers, even if it involved a certain amount of ribbing, they had a natural and fair-minded spirit, which differs greatly from that found in the soft lounges of the politically correct.

"There was a good cultural mix, though Irish was the dominant culture," says Father Williams. "I remember when I went to college people thought I was odd because of my favourite foods. I liked salt-fish, pig's belly, trotters, even flukes, winkles and cockles, because that was what I ate at home.

"The mixing of different traditions was stronger in this part of Liverpool. But it was the sense of community which has been sustained into a feeling of nostalgia. All my aunties and uncles belonged to the same parish and all four grandparents were born on Scotland Road."

Can the appeal of old Scottie Road be more widely understood? "It was deeply attached to the Roman Catholic Church," says Steve Binns, community historian with Liverpool City Council. "Its relationship to the city establishment has always been tenuous and sometimes strained. The road came to symbolise a certain type of Liverpudlian. The area was poor but it had an absolute cohesiveness. You could call it pride. It is that old sense of the outsider, going against the grain, beyond the pale, struggling all the time against various things. It had that frontier town image which stayed with it."

THE SPIRIT OF THE PEOPLE

They say there is a little bit of Scotland Road everywhere in the world. Well, to the cynic, that might seem like the dewy-eyed claim of men and women who will always be passionate about the 'auld' back-to-back terraces. There, they scabbed their knees and dried the drips from noses when the fog, falling from belching chimneys, made everything grey, and the acrid smell of charcoal rose from the alleys. But they are not talking only of the packed rubble and the tar they laid over it as the generations passed on. For Scotland Road, perhaps more than any other address in Britain, was built on the spirit of its people.

Those people travelled the world on the big ships that left Liverpool. The long corridor walked by the crew was invariably known as Scotland Road because everything ran off it. This was true even of the *Titanic*. Of course, when they were ashore, the men carried their special ways with them, telling total strangers of how things were done at home. Thus, the poorest quarter of Liverpool came to colonise the world.

Nobody is prouder of that heritage than Ron Formby, editor of the monthly *Scottie Press*, which continues to sell about 2,500 copies even though the old community has been greatly reduced by clearance programmes and new developments. In fact, Ron rejects the title of editor. "I just put it together," he says, as the steam from another cup of tea rises to his lips in his office in the Vauxhall Multiservices Centre, Silvester Street.

The *Scottie Press* began in 1971 and is now the longest-running community newspaper in Britain. Ron does most of it himself – leaping hither and thither in his brown leather bomber jacket – the writing, the photographs and the page lay-outs, though articles are contributed by local historians and authors like Terry Cooke and Mike Kelly. The next ambition of Ron and all involved with the centre is to organise the 200th anniversary celebrations. Many believe that it would be appropriate for the descendants of the community, which suffered so much in the making of Liverpool, to whoop-it-up for one grand night in the Town Hall or St George's Hall. It would be a night of nights, beneath the chandeliers, when those who made it big in the world would be at one again with those who failed. Once they knew the same bricks and saw the same skyline, when everyone had high ambitions.

The emphasis of all this will be on the 'ordinary' people, but the anniversary will also be an opportunity to celebrate the famous Italian fish-fryers, like the Gianelli and Podesta families, the politicians and the entertainers. The Vauxhall History and Heritage Group has been producing memorial plaques to honour some of the local heroes.

There was Billy Collins, 5ft 5in and stocky, the man who started the inter-street football league in 1953. Each season ended with a cup final played on an asphalt pitch, lit by gas lamps on Limekiln Lane. Billy died six years ago, but the contribution he made to local football continues. Among the fine players were Jimmy Melia (England, Liverpool, Wolves, Southampton and Crewe), Larry Carberry (Ipswich and Barrow) and Bobby Campbell (Liverpool, Portsmouth and Aldershot).

Another great 'fellah' remembered on a plaque is Jim Clarke, who came to Liverpool as a stowaway on board a ship from Georgetown, British Guiana. Although few black people had settled in the area, Jim's charming manners soon won admirers. "We never thought of him as black, he was one of us," they said. But it was as a swimmer that he made his name, rescuing dozens of children who had fallen in the 'scaldies' – a stretch of the Leeds/Liverpool Canal heated by the boiling water flushed there after it had been used in the refining process at the Tate and Lyle sugar factory.

Outside the city, though, most people associate Scotland Road with Cilla Black, the daughter of a market-stall holder and docker, who became a famous singer and later the hostess of TV shows like *Blind Date*. Christened Priscilla Maria Veronica White, she was raised at number 380, next to a Chinese laundry and above Murray the barber. Despite criticism from some quarters, and one of the most mimicked voices in showbiz ('Lorra Lorra'), Cilla has survived triumph and tragedy. Her husband and sweetheart, Bobby Willis, died in 1999. There was a tough streak in the old girl of St Anthony's School, who was introduced to the greenery and agricultural smells at 14 when she was sent pea-picking in Lydiate.

Perhaps the most eloquent politicians on Scotland Road never had a public platform. Instead, they put the world to rights with the lipstick girls, the philosophers with flapping soles, the shadow boxers, the dockers with daughters in university, and the gambling 'professors' with stubby pencils and shine on their suits, whose 'certs' could fall to the back of the field in the burning of a self-rolled cigarette. They met in pubs with magnificent names such as the Foot Hospital (291 Scotland Road), the Rotunda Vaults (397) and the Throstles Nest (still open at number 344). But the names of three 'real' politicians, who represented the old Scotland Division of Liverpool in the Commons, stand out.

Thomas Power O'Connor was known as 'Tay Pay' during a parliamentary career of 49 years, 44 of which were spent as the member for the Scotland Division, leading to him becoming Father of the House. O'Connor (1849-1929) was born in Athlone, where he was educated at the College of the Immaculate Conception before advancing to Queen's College, Galway, where he received his MA. Although Tay Pay's true strength lay in journalism, his advocacy of Irish Nationalism, though unpopular in other parts of the UK, stood him in good stead in his constituency. In the General Election of 1918, two years after the Easter Uprising, Tay Pay was elected unopposed, which tells us much about the sympathies of people in that part of Liverpool. Away from politics, he wrote biographies of Napoleon, Disraeli and Charles Stewart Parnell, and founded radical newspapers including *TP's Weekly* and *TP's Journal*.

'Dandy' Patrick Byrne was a city councillor and landlord of the Morning Star pub. Much later, the Irish leader Eamon De Valera was reported to have been sheltered there on his way to the USA after escaping gaol in 1918. Dandy, who died in 1890, was always elegantly dressed in a seel-skin vest and white topper. His generosity to the poor was legendary, so a fountain to his memory was erected by his customers. It was re-dedicated in the grounds of St Anthony's Church, Scotland Road, in 2000.

Bessie Braddock (née Bamber) was born in Zante Street in 1899. She entered the Commons as the Labour MP for the Scotland/Exchange seat in 1945, serving the people with a steadfast will until the illness that ended her life in 1970. In the popular press, Bessie was seen as the mother of all fighting Liverpudlians, always siding with the underdog, never respecting authority. They mourned her in their thousands, remembering always that formidable jaw wobbling with indignation.

Now Ron is winding his legs around each other on the editor's chair. He's a modest man and won't say it himself, but the day will come when they will want to celebrate him, as they have celebrated the others who have done so much for the area. Fifty-five-year-old Ron and his brother William were brought up in a terraced house in Stanley Road. His mother, Patricia, began as a pools checker, later becoming a telephonist like her husband, William. In 1982, Ron, then a carpet salesman, came to the Vauxhall Multiservices centre to study for an English O Level, but he soon began helping with the *Scottie Press*, taking photographs and contributing articles. When he was made redundant, the paper became a full-time job.

"Two thousand and three is a symbolic year in the lives of the old Scottie Roaders," says Ron. "You have to be honest and say that this will be the last opportunity most of them will have of celebrating a big anniversary. This will be an official celebration, an opportunity for people to be recognised as Scottie Roaders. But the city of Liverpool will also have the chance to recognise Scottie Road as its spiritual home. It is so important to remember how diverse the culture of the area is, now that Liverpool has put in its bid to be the European Capital of Culture [which it won]. I know this sounds nice, and you can get the violin out, but Scotland Road is in every country in the world. To think of it as a strip of rubble and tarmac is to miss its soul. You had the A to Z of people here. Some were on skid row, others were doing quite well. It all came together on Scotland Road."

VICTORIAN LIVERPOOL

THE FIGHTER: JEM MACE

Hard men laid flowers before the headstone just erected in memory of England's last bare-knuckle boxing champion of the world.

Jem Mace had been buried in a plot in Anfield Cemetery, Liverpool, on 6 December 1910, but no name had marked his grave, only a number – 594. How that end contrasted with the day when Jem visited Liverpool in 1866 to celebrate his victory over the legendary Joe Goss. A crowd of more than 10,000 greeted him, all singing, *For He's a Jolly Good Fellow*. They lifted Jem's ten-and-a-half stone body and chaired him shoulder high to a civic reception, where seven dozen bottles of champagne were poured into a silver vessel and supped enthusiastically.

Yesterday, just 12 members of the Merseyside Former Boxers' Association attended the ceremony as wind and rain lashed the Church of England cemetery. The men had decided that there should be a permanent memorial to Jem, who is regarded by experts as the father of modern boxing because he confused slower-witted opponents with his dancing, fast fists, feinting and masterful defensive tactics. So they began collecting until they had the £640 needed for the stone of polished black granite to be shaped and inscribed.

The wreath was placed by Harry Scott, a middleweight amateur champion, who turned professional in the early 1960s. During this time, Scott fought Reuben Carter, who was later featured in Bob Dylan's song *The Hurricane*. It claimed that Carter had been wrongly convicted for the killing of three men in a bungled robbery. Whatever the truth of that, Carter was one of the most feared men in the ring. Scott and Carter's first meeting was stopped after ten rounds. Blood was gushing from one of Scott's eyes, but he out-pointed Carter over the distance on their return. Yesterday, though, Harry's thoughts were all for Jem, the fighter who toughened his fists by 'pickling' them in a solution of whisky, gunpowder and hedgehog fat to prevent bruising and swelling.

Gently, Harry Scott rested on his haunches to read the inscription to Jem before raising himself up again, a little stiffly. The silver inscription is taken from a poem left on the graveside when Jem was buried. The men, some with eyes puffed and noses broken by their own times in the ring, read the words:

> *Where hardy heroes nature's weapons wield.*
> *He stood unconquered, champion of the field.*
> *Time counts him out. But memory will remain.*
> *We ne'er will look upon his like again.*

Jem was born in the village of Beeston, Norfolk, on 8 April 1831. Although he denied being a Gypsy, he came from a travelling family. Young men sharpened their skills against all-comers in the boxing booths. At 5ft 9in tall, Jem compensated for his slight build with courage and guile. His promise as a fighter was first observed outside a pub where he had been playing the fiddle to entertain the locals, when three drunken thugs tried to interrupt the performance. One grabbed the violin and smashed it on the ground. Two of his tormentors fell like skittles as Jem gave the crowd an exhibition of the finer points of pugilism. That done, he blew on his knuckles and lifted the broken violin. The third man fled as the crowd began a collection.

As his prize-fighting reputation grew, Jem took on all the stars, felling Sam Hurst on 18 June 1861 to claim the English Championship. He lost it to Tom King the following year, but the fight had been so fierce that King declined a return, thus surrendering the title to Jem. In 1870, he became the World Champion under Prize Ring Rules, defeating Tom Allen, the American number one, over ten rounds in Kennerville, Louisiana. At the height of his fame, he owned a fairground known as the Strawberry Gardens, in the Breckfield Road area of Anfield. His fame as a boxer took him around the world. On a visit to Australia, he paraded his skills for ten guineas before three bush rangers. One was the notorious Ned Kelly.

In 1954, Jem entered the international Boxing Hall of Fame to join such immortals as John L Sullivan, Bob Fitzsimmons, Jack Dempsey, Joe Louis, Rocky Marciano and Muhammad Ali.

He was giving exhibition bouts until shortly before his death. He died of 'pneumonia and senile decay' in the Victoria Hotel, Jarrow, a few months short of his 80th birthday. His body was sent to Liverpool and tributes were received from all over the world.

Although he was penniless at his death, Jem had lost and won many fortunes on his way to a kind of immortality. "I was tremendously honoured to be asked to do his headstone," said John Smith, the managing director of Crosby Memorials.

Jim Jenkinson, registrar of the Merseyside Former Boxers' Association, said: "Jem was illiterate but he could read an opponent's style. Photographs were taken of him two years before he died and there was not a mark on him. He had a perfect nose and no cauliflower ears, which was remarkable in a bare-fist fighter."

"He should be remembered. He was a world champion, simple as that," said Harry Scott.

ATHOL STREET POLICE STATION

They were big men, often hardened by army service, but their compassion and understanding of street justice made them the true friends of needy people. Now a commemorative plaque is to be laid on the site of the old Athol Street police station, Liverpool, where it was said that the bobbies knew every nook and cranny and every crook and nanny. They had to then, because they were serving the city's Scotland Road area, one of the toughest neighbourhoods in the UK.

There, in the fog of winter, ragged children emerged like little ghosts as they scurried the pavements, bare-footed, carrying pots of ale from the pubs to the hovels of their parents. The drink spawned crime and violence but the tall policemen, walking in pairs and looking like giants, often well over six-feet high in their conical helmets, noticed a cowering child or a bruised wife. "We should visit that home," they said, to one another. Armed with only their truncheons, a whistle and a lantern, the officers set about bringing order to the streets.

Liverpool's police force began in 1836. Athol Street was its second station, following the one at Exchange. The station, with its six, four-bed cells, was built by Liverpool Police in 1855 amid disease-soaked streets and courtyards packed with Irish people who had fled the Potato Famine. Locally, it was known as the bridewell because it had overnight accommodation for 'guests' awaiting trial for offences. The offences usually involved violence, drunkenness and theft, or all three. The sergeant and his family had rooms upstairs – a sensible arrangement as it allowed his wife to search female prisoners. On a Saturday night, the line of policemen leading wrong-doers towards the charge-desk was a kind of underworld equivalent of the gentry queuing for the opera.

About 60 officers were based at the station. Villains and law-abiding citizens alike respected the police officers of Athol Street, many of whom had served in the armed forces. If you had gone over the top at the Somme, or one of the other slaughter-fields of World War I, even the fast-fisted alley-runners of Scotland Road didn't seem so menacing. The medals worn by these men were a symbol of their bravery, immediately exciting the admiration of their fellow citizens. The tradition continued after the wars to the brink of the modern age.

Terry Cooke, chairman of the Vauxhall History and Heritage Group which has commissioned the plaque, was brought up on William Moult Street, opposite the police station in the city's D Division. Terry and his sister Mary and brother Joseph were the children of a coppersmith, Edward, and his wife Johanna. They grew up hearing about such bobbies as Musical and Baby Face – most of the Athol Street officers were given nicknames.

"Athol Street was built to accommodate drunk and violent prisoners," said Terry. "At the time it was commissioned, hundreds of bare-foot children were walking the streets at night, begging. The beat bobby had a great deal of compassion for the children and their parents." In this way, the officers were accepted by the residents. Women whose husbands were away would sometimes ask a policeman to speak to their growing sons before they got into serious trouble.

On occasions, an individual policeman might deal with a situation on his own, without recourse to the courts. One officer heard a little girl in rags whimpering behind an ash-bin. The drunken stepfather had leathered the girl with his belt after she had tried to stop him battering her mother. The stepfather improved in all sorts of ways after a visit from the bobby.

Terry explained more about the officers' nicknames. "Many had nicknames," he said. "In the nineteen thirties, there was Musical, a member of the police band who was always whistling, and Baby Face, a handsome but young-looking man. In an effort to change his image, Baby Face grew a handlebar moustache, but the girls told him to shave it off. He did. Those men knew the most important part of community policing – making contact with the public."

Of course, community policing is back in fashion. Bob Leyland is 49 and retires next month after 30 years with the force. He is based at Stanley Road station, where he is community officer for the old Athol Street area. He said, "In the old days we were 'scuffers', and then we became 'busies' because whenever a prisoner called for something from his cell, the officer would say, 'I'm busy'. But the main thing is that we're all community police officers."

From 1895 until about 1946, the officers voluntarily donated to the Police Aided Clothing Association. This provided the children with clogs, corduroy suits and rough cloth dresses. Among the contributors was PC Tony Mari who plodded the beat for the 30 years up to his retirement in 1963. Twenty-three years later, hundreds attended his funeral.

"That in itself was a tribute to the beat bobby and the place he had in the community," said Terry. "The plaque dedicated to the memory of men like that will go on the site of the station, which is now an old folk's home. That is appropriate in itself because people there will have memories of the old beat bobbies."

Athol Street station was demolished in 1967 as part of the clearance programmes that broke up the old Scotland Road community. Terry and many others firmly believe we should always remember the importance that the stout brick building had in those days, when policemen were friends to people engaged in a ceaseless struggle against adversity.

THE 'SACK-'EM-UP' MEN

A gruesome tale about trafficking in bodies from Liverpool and the subsequent creation of the unpopular Anatomy Act 168 years ago. It was written in February 2001 when Liverpool was still recoiling in shock and grief from the news that body parts at Alder Hey had been used for medical research without the consent of the deceased children's next of kin.

~

A whisker of thread tying together the toes of a wretched woman, led to the discovery that a cellar in Liverpool had been used as a warehouse for the dead. In the murk could be seen a scattering of sacks and barrels filled with the bodies of 22 men, women and children. The police surgeon, Thomas William Davis, stepped amongst the silent assembly, periodically placing a scented handkerchief to his nostrils as he rolled over a corpse, wondering why it had been laid in the bricked dampness beneath the apparently respectable home of a man of God. There was no obvious evidence to suggest that any of the bodies had suffered injury before death. Then his keen eyes spotted the thread. In those days, bodies were often tied by the feet before burial.

It seemed impossible – something from the twisted roots of depraved imagination – but could the people before him have been disinterred? Davis' fears were confirmed when his torch glinted on a syringe of the sort used by anatomists to pump hot wax into the veins and arteries of cadavers.

This was October 1826, two years before the case of William Burke and William Hare was brought before Edinburgh High Court and polite society learnt for the first time of the activities of men variously described as body-snatchers, grave-robbers or the resurrectionists. In Liverpool's grim underworld, however, 'sack 'em-up men' was the favoured term for the figures who frequented cemeteries at night by the light of guttering candles, removing fresh corpses from their shallow graves so that they could be sold to anatomists.

Davies was unearthing the secrets of the sackmen beneath the rooms that were used by the Reverend James Macgowan as a school for gentlefolk. In January of that year, a mysterious man, calling himself John Henderson, and supposedly a cooper from Greenock, had moved into the basement to further his business in the export of fish oil. To these premises, Davis was called after the crew and passengers had complained of a foul stench from a row of barrels loaded on to the *Latona*, which was berthed at the Pier Head.

These casks supposedly housed salted hides, but Captain Walker decided to examine one. As he removed a plug, one of the barrels burst open and a body pitched out in a cascade of salt. Eleven corpses were found in this 'cargo', which had been bound for Glasgow and then on to the Medical School at Edinburgh where the one-eyed Dr Robert Knox was a popular anatomist, drawing to his dramatic lectures more than 500 people, including students, artists and writers.

Knox's need for bodies exceeded the supply that could be legally provided. Officially, each medical school was only allowed the body of one executed criminal or suicide per year. Burke and Hare saw a gap in the market. A fresh corpse could fetch £10 or £15, depending on freshness, and no questions asked. So the pair from Ireland teamed up with Helen McDougal and a woman called Margaret, who took Hare's surname without recourse to marriage.

In the early days, the gang courteously waited for their subjects to die before flogging them to the medics. Later, driven by greed, they decided to increase their turnover by killing people whose disappearances were unlikely to be reported to the authorities – prostitutes, tramps and drifters. Drink was invariably the enticement. When the victim had sunk into a stupor, the women would withdraw and either Burke or Hare would 'bring the matter to a conclusion'. Between February and October 1828, it is estimated that 16 people were disposed of in this way, though their final tally might have reached 30.

The four operated in one of the vilest slum areas of Edinburgh, then known as Auld Reekie, and the police had difficulty building a case against them. Finally, though, they were charged with murdering an old Irish woman, Mrs Docherty.

In keeping with his devious character, Hare turned King's evidence. Burke was found guilty and hanged on 29 January 1829. His stout but short body, topped with sandy whiskers and sunken eyes, was salted for 'useful dissecting' and transported to the Edinburgh Medical School, where he joined his victims in a ghastly union. Burke's skeleton now hangs in the museum at Edinburgh University's department of anatomy.

Hare was recognised by workmen after his release in February and they flung him into a pit of quicklime where he was blinded. Although he survived Burke by 40 years, Hare never saw another body. Nannies in the street would point at him and warn their children never to go near him.

Dr Knox the anatomist was not charged with any offence and he lived until 1862. Revered by some as a man whose research has widened medical knowledge about the human body and its workings, he was hated by others.

The use of body parts in research was then, as now, a sensitive subject. The names of Burke and Hare will dwell forever in infamy. From their dreadful deeds, however, emerged the controversial Anatomy Act of 1832, which allowed hospitals to use the corpses of the poor instead of having to depend upon stolen ones. Before then, only corpses from the gallows could be legally dissected. The body of anyone given a pauper's funeral could now be handed over for medical research without argument. It was one of the most socially divisive pieces of legislation ever passed.

Many religions maintained that the body was needed to enable one to pass into the next life. Christians clung to their belief in the resurrection of the body and the life everlasting. Even so, most denominations had accepted cremations by the late nineteenth century. The Roman Catholic ban on cremations was not relaxed until 1963.

Liverpool's part in the supply of bodies to Knox and the other anatomists far exceeded the 11 found on the ship and the 22 in the cellar, all taken from the parish cemetery in Cambridge Street. From that investigation, three people were charged with carrying bodies from their graves. During the trial of 25-year-old James Donaldson, the court was told of a huge barrel of babies being soaked in brine. Court officials shuddered and the foreman of the jury was taken ill. Yet Donaldson was sentenced to only 12 months in prison and ordered to pay a £50 fine. Another two men charged with the same offence were also sent to prison for just a year and ordered to pay fines of £21.

In Liverpool, many grieving widows and widowers, mothers and fathers, must have knelt in remembrance, unaware that they were laying flowers over empty graves. They belonged to a generation of profound faith.

Although medical science has advanced greatly and beliefs have changed, society remains uncertain about how the human body should retain its dignity once earthly life has ended. The activities of Dick van Velzen, the former pathologist at the centre of the Alder Hey Hospital scandal, remind us that it is the feelings of the living which are exposed and hurt when we dispose of the dead without due care and respect.

So unpopular was the Anatomy Act, it directly led to the introduction in Victorian times of the insurance industry, which enabled the poor to provide themselves with a decent funeral and avoid the ignominy of their bodies being used for medical research without their consent.

VILLAGE LIFE

DERBY VILLAGE.

In the crazy spin of today's world, many hope to find peace in rural places. Merseyside has many fine old villages. I'm a townie myself, but the robust smells of the country have a certain appeal to me. I particularly enjoy the smells of raw spirits and tobacco smoke found in all self-respecting village inns. These snapshots of the hidden villages of Merseyside all first appeared in Autumn 2001.

WEST DERBY

With the first chilled wind of winter lifting the grey of her hair, Frankla Corris looks as doughty a representative of the village breed as you are likely to find. At her prime, when she chalked the blackboard in the church school, Frankla stood at 5ft 10in, but the passing years have shaved her height a little. Her spirit, though, continues to grow.

Now she is standing in a tartan skirt before the railings around the local pillory. A poppy hangs vividly from the lapel of her quilted coat, in memory and pride. She has lived in this village of West Derby since girlhood and believes its history should live on in the hearts of the new villagers, as it did for her generation. Her lips stretch in humour when she tells of how merry-makers once tweaked the noses of the wretches whose hands and heads were secured in the original pillory, staked on this spot, opposite the old courtroom. Those poor fellows were not major miscreants, but hen-thieves, drunks and serfs whose careless agricultural activities had muddied the water supply.

Popular myth may suggest they were pelted with eggs and tomatoes while paraded to public mockery. The scholarly 84-year-old widow disagrees. Tomatoes and eggs were expensive; a tweak on the nose was free. The victim, of course, could do little other than squeal his displeasure. But to suffer such ignominy in the full flush of a hangover must have served as a stern warning to the young. The pillory was abolished as a form of punishment in 1837, but commemorative stocks were erected in the village in 1904, so that people would remember how it was.

The Grade II courthouse is the oldest building in the village. Although the present structure was restored for £40 under the warrant on Elizabeth I in 1586, the reeve had held courts there since Norse times, possibly as early as the reign of Alfred the Great (AD 949-999). With a jury of 12, the court also appointed such local dignitaries as the bread and ale tasters. "To make sure there wasn't too much sugar in the ale, they poured some on a bench and sat a man there in leather trousers," Frankla said. "If he stuck, there was too much sugar."

This is ancient England. Thonged-sandals dragged hoes over the rich mud here. The name Derby was used by the Vikings to describe the place of the 'deor' (deer). Soon they had a 'wapentake', an early court where verdicts would be given by the raising of spears. The court was also the administrative centre for the whole of

West Derby, which became a royal hunting estate, stretching from the Ribble to the Mersey, embracing many small communities, including Liverpool. The village was the capital of this vast area. Locals boast of its pre-eminence over Liverpool. The evidence is in the *Domesday Book*, the land survey carried out in 1086 for William the Conqueror.

With the Normans came the Molyneux family, later to become the Earls of Sefton (motto: To Conquer is to Live), whose home was Croxteth Hall. It was acquired by Liverpool City Council in 1972 when the seventh Lord Sefton (Hugh Molyneux) died childless.

Old-timers remember the heavy stride of his brogues crunching the leaves that fell profusely around the sandstone Church of St Mary the Angel. Sefton was a popular figure in society magazines and, at 6ft 4in, was regarded as the handsomest man in the House of Lords. With his red-haired American wife, Josephine, he hobnobbed with Edward III during his courting days with Wallis Simpson. In the later, quieter years, however, he was happy to acknowledge the nods of villagers, one of whom was young Stephen Guy, now chairman of the West Derby Society, who remembers buying gold fish in a plastic bag from the village pet shop and exercising them in the basin of the fountain erected in honour of temperance in front of the village cross.

Above the mosaic face of the fountain are carved the words, 'Water is Best', which offered a confident taunt to the surrounding pubs, the Hare and Hounds, the Sefton Arms and the West Derby. However, the demon drink prevailed and the fountain has not squirted for many years.

Stephen is more concerned about the fruit shop over the road. An application to turn it into a bookmakers was rejected by Liverpool City Council, which is now considering an appeal against the decision. Stephen's society has joined with the West Derby Village Residents and Business Association in opposing the plan.

These days, the courthouse is maintained by the city council as a place of historic interest and is squeezed between a flower shop and Chu's Chinese takeaway. Almost opposite is the Yeoman's house, also built in the 1580s. Most of the village, contained in a small conservation area, is Victorian, but the society and association concern themselves with the past and present, acting together to protect the old village while monitoring the changes that will ensure its future. For example, there is the restoration of the memorial built for the 125 locals who gave their lives "for righteousness and peace" in World War I, and at the back of the church is a Millennium Centre for community gatherings, opened this year by the Duchess of Gloucester.

Now, Frankla and Stephen have joined John Kennedy, chairman of the residents' association, and Jack Cooper, for a walk to the rectory, passing by the 160ft tower of the church which was designed in the 1850s in the grand Gothic style by Gilbert Scott. Jack, a retired headmaster, wrote a book called the *History of West Derby* with his pal David Power.

Rector Roger Wikeley and his wife Geraldine have been here for 16 years, raising their children Jonathan, a music student aged 22, and 13-year-old Katherine. "When I came here I thought this was just a suburb," said Roger. "But it is a real village with a very village-like feel and you are not here long before you know that."

Nobody knows it better than Frankla, who has taught at both the village schools, St Mary's and the Catholic St Peter's. Her husband John died 20 years ago and they had no children. "But I have had more children than anyone else here," she said, "thousands of them." They are the boys and girls she guided through school into the village of today.

WOOLTON VILLAGE

Under the stone sleeps Eleanor Rigby, forever unaware her name gave the world a song to sing about the loneliness of the night. Along the way a little, through the wet grass of the graveyard, by those forgotten and those remembered fondly, lies Bob Paisley, a man who knew something of earthly triumph.

In a lounge, not far away, Janet Gnosspelius, architect, historian and stalwart of the village society, sucks the tip of her long cigarette-holder, before gazing from the window of her post-war semi. The rain drifts down from the hill over her garden.

Today 75-year-old Miss Gnosspelius is dressed in a sensible, brown tweed skirt and there is a confident knot in the yellow of her tie. Before her, on the table, are the maps of old Woolton and a magnifying glass so she can better scrutinise the places and names that form this village she so loves. The late eighteenth century clock in the corner tick-tocks to the unflinching rhythm that marks the passing of her days. To people of quick judgement, she may appear eccentric, but this is a lady of determined scholarship, proud to speak of her grandfather Adolphus who came to these parts from Stockholm in 1844, hoping to make a fortune from cotton. Her father was the redoubtable Oscar Theodor Gnosspelius, a widely travelled civil engineer and flying pioneer, who, before World War I, produced the first monoplane to take-off and land on Lake Windermere. By the clock is her ancient Wilcox and Gibbs sewing machine, which whirrs along to the prompting of the treadle. "Oh, it's a marvellous little beast," says Miss Gnosspelius. "I'll say it still works! It was my grandmother's."

What has she been making? "I have just made myself a new pair of pants," she says with a nod, and a half-smile puckers her chin. "And I am going to make myself a new skirt, too." This is because her ginger cat, Max, has been stretching his claws in the weave of her present skirt. Now, to history. She speaks slowly and deliberately about her village.

In 1975, Miss Gnosspelius and John Lally published *The History of Woolton*. Its height – about 300ft at the summit – gave locals a fine view of the Welsh hills as well as the surrounding country. Archaeological evidence suggests there was an Iron Age lookout base on Camp Hill as early as 150BC. The name Woolton derives from that of Wulfa, an Anglo Saxon landowner, and tun (the old English name for settlement). It is listed in the *Domesday Book* as the townships of Uluentune (Little Woolton) and Uuetone (Much Woolton).

In 1178, John, Constable of Chester and Baron of Halton and Widnes, granted Much Woolton to the Knights Hospitaliers, of the Order of St John, who had founded a hospital in Jerusalem for Christian pilgrims. Soon afterwards, Little Woolton fell under the guardianship of the Cistercians based at Stanlow Abbey. However, by 1203, after some disputes, it, too, was also held by the Hospitaliers. The fact that Woolton was a place of some account can be seen in the fourteenth century village cross.

In 1704, Richard Molyneux, son of William, Viscount Molyneux of Croxteth, began expanding a substantial farmhouse into Woolton Hall, now a Masonic hall used for private parties and functions. Woolton was really little more than an agricultural hamlet until the nineteenth century. In 1801, the population of Much Woolton was 439. Fifty years later it was 3,669. The sudden increase is explained by the arrival of Irish people fleeing the potato famine, and the growing importance of Liverpool.

Many Irishmen laboured in the quarries. The sandstone, with its distinctive pink flush, was extensively used in the cladding of Liverpool Cathedral. Others found employment on farms, in building Garston docks and railway, or as servants in the grander houses. They crowded into small streets, bringing a new culture to the old village.

Down on Church Road, Woolton, polished oak planks are being laid in the floor of a Georgian cottage owned by 54-year-old John Ashton, North West regional director of public health and chairman of the 500-strong Woolton Society. He shares the house with his partner, Maggi Morris and a skeleton, whose bones he is now rattling. "From student days," he explains. This man's big brother David once fought John Lennon over a football in the cow-fields on Reservoir Road. Who won the fight? "Depends on whom you talk to," replied diplomatic John. He is talking about the village while we walk towards St Peter's Church Hall, where John Lennon first met Paul McCartney on 6 July 1957.

"This is a fabulous environment," he says. "We have got woods, playing fields, golf courses, the Woolton Cinema, the swimming baths (believed to be the first in Liverpool), a library, pubs, the village club where you play snooker."

Litter was a problem in the village. So, after complaints from the Woolton Society, the city council sent in veteran sweeper Tony Sarmin with his barrow and paper-picker. "I have been here since July and love the job," he says. "If there was eight days in the week, I'd work them. I have been brushing in Liverpool for thirty-one years."

Down Quarry Street, Bernie Blackmore, a 70-year-old farrier and blacksmith, is sitting in his office. His father Frank began the business after the Great War, and his son Paul is continuing the family tradition. Bernie began the seven-year apprenticeship before joining the horse transport section of the Royal Army Service Corps. The high moment of his life as a private came with the Coronation in 1953, when he was a footman with the horses pulling the carriage of Louis Stephen St Laurent, the Canadian Prime Minister. "I was very pleased about that," he recalls.

Back in the graveyard, tourists are photographing the stone which tells that Eleanor Rigby died on 10 October 1939. They chatter away. Nobody sings the song. There are those, however, who sing for Eleanor, in the dark, after the barmaid has folded the towel over the beer taps.

Bob Paisley's son, Graham Paisley, sees the people come and go. He is the verger of the church where his father was laid to rest in 1996. Of his father – the most successful manager in English football history – he says fondly, "He remained an ordinary man amid extraordinary achievements."

KNOWSLEY VILLAGE

The canon is what seasoned folk would call a 'brick', a jolly old soul. In a green blouse and tartan trews, she gives an evangelical vent to a good hymn, and the old pipe organ wheezes along with admirable gusto in the sandstone church. However, some parishioners are worried about the condition of the steeple. Along with the apple trees and the memories, the steeple dominates life in Knowsley Village. It seems the iron skeleton is corroding and this is causing it to swell, splitting the exterior stone. Something will have to be done. It's a problem for the 53-year-old canon, Cynthia Dowdle, but she discusses it in no-nonsense language with rolling vowels redolent of her girlhood on an 84-acre farm near Ormskirk where her parents, Charles and Joan, grew potatoes, cabbages and sprouts.

"Some of the sandstone is actually cracked," she says. "Now, we have got to find two hundred thousand pounds to repair it. There is an English Heritage Lottery grant of seventy thousand, four hundred pounds, but before we can use that, we have to raise an equal amount ourselves. It's a lot, but we raised seven thousand on our Gift Day from the immediate church family. Now we need help from the wider family; people who have left the area or had a wedding or baptism here."

To everyone in these parts, Cynthia is simply the vicar. In days preserved by sepia images, every English village had a vicar. Preparing the Sunday sermon in his head as he wandered the green in the warm of late afternoon, pausing under a tree to applaud good play by the cricketers; he bowled a mean googly himself, when he was a young man. Cynthia, of course, comes from a different age. To begin with, she's a woman, a fact that would not have escaped the keen gaze of Agatha Christie's Jane Marple, sleuth of St Mary Mead. What's more, she's a canon as well, a couple of notches up on the Anglican pecking order, but Cynthia's not one to concern herself about such matters.

Comparisons with the BBC's *Vicar of Dibley*, played by the comedienne Dawn French, are inevitable. "There have been comments, especially since I have grown my hair a bit longer," she says, before laughing them off. Her devotion to God, though, is serious.

"I went on this pilgrimage to the Holy Land," she says. "When I was on the shores of Lake Galilee, I had a real feeling of God's presence. I was reading the passage from John when Jesus asks Peter: 'Do you love me?' I actually heard the Lord say, 'Cynthia, do you love me?' and I said, 'You know I do'. Then he said, 'Take care of my sheep'."

That was 1984. At the time, Cynthia was a teacher and she felt she could pursue her faith in the primary schools where she worked and she progressed to a headship at St Mary's, Eccleston. "But there was still this frustration in me," she says. "I wanted to do more." These were the days before the ordination of women. Becoming a deaconess was the height of female ambition, until the reactionary element in the Church made it yield some ground and allowed women to be deacons. Cynthia studied theology at St John's College, Durham, coming out as a deacon in 1990 to work at All Hallows Church, Allerton. Two years later, the General Synod voted in favour of women becoming priests, and, on 29 May 1994, Cynthia was ordained at Liverpool Cathedral. From All Hallows, she was appointed team rector at Halewood.

She arrived at St Mary the Virgin, Knowsley, in February of last year. The church was built between 1841 and 1844 with £20,000 donated by Edward Stanley, the 13th Earl of Derby. His family owned the area and built its schools, cottages and, in 1897, the village hall. Cynthia had joined an ancient place of worship. Research done by Henry Dams, village vicar from 1910 to 1928, unearthed the twelfth century Chapel of St Leonard on land which was granted to the Earl of Derby in 1553. There were also chapels in Knowsley Hall, the ancestral seat of the Stanley family.

Cynthia holds a *Book of Common Prayer* service early each Sunday, followed by the family service at 11am. The church still fills to its 200-capacity quite regularly. There are children and the elderly in the congregation, but very few people in their 20s and 30s. The village's population fell from 3,206 in 1991 to 3,097 in 1995.

She is talking by the marble tomb of three times Prime Minister, Edward, the 14th Earl of Derby, who was born in 1799 and died in 1869. On the opposite wall is a wonderful mosaic depicting scenes of the Angel at the Annunciation, the Nativity, the Kings bearing gifts, and four angels. The church and its opulent fittings represent the influence of one powerful family, but at the Harvest Festival, humbler villagers laid their offerings from God's earth outside the vestry – potatoes, carrots, cabbages, just like those grown by Cynthia's own father.

Modern houses, costing up to £200,000, face the cottages of the old community, but Cynthia says, "This is still very much a village community. A lot of people have lived here all their lives. There is still a feeling of caring." She likes to walk her Jack Russell terrier called Sally down from the vicarage to Tithebarn Road.

Peggy Ashton and her husband Jack are old villagers. Peggy's father, Charles Wheeler, was the coachman and then chauffeur to Lord Derby. Jack's father, Robert Atherton, worked at Pear Tree Farm, Kirkby, for Lord Sefton. They live in the cottage taken by Peggy's family in 1948.

"I remember the agent telling my parents that he was terribly sorry, but they would have to charge them four shillings (twenty pence) a week rent," she says. "But that was security, so we would never be turned out." Tenants on the Derby's estate had paid no rent. With the house came a lovely garden of almost an acre.

"Oh, we have so much wildlife – hundreds of birds, hedgehogs, squirrels, foxes," she says, staring into the distance as the leaves of autumn fall on her soft lawn. "I used to love gardening, but I can't do much now because of my arthritis. I had a hip replacement, but it has spread to my back," says Peggy, who was a land girl during the war, bottling in a dairy. She married Jack in 1955 and he moved into the house, which had been built 100 years earlier.

Peggy and Jack stand together under the vines. They never had children. In the garden there is an old spreading oak that has stood firm through the generations. "When we came here, my father took an acorn from his waistcoat pocket and put it in the ground," she says, smiling. "He said, 'We'll plant this here and see if it grows'."

It did.

OXTON VILLAGE

The village wakes early. In the blue villas with their stucco walls, men and women are lying beneath high ceilings. They do not stir and have yet to rinse the stale taste of sleep from their mouths, but the black cats that have prowled in the night and wailed their passions to the skies are stretching and licking their paws on the cobbled alleys in front of the little sandstone terraces. Here, they still have bars for gentlemen to rub the mud from their shoes. There's a bright sound of metal shutters rolling up on the shops around which village life will soon gather. Colin Farquhar has parked his blue van and he is laying boxes of fruit and vegetables on the racks outside the entrance. Soon, the milkman and the breadman will arrive and deliver supplies to the Village Green general store. The door opens, its bell rings. Colin rubs the back of his hand on his grizzled chin and walks towards the till. It is 7am.

A few yards away, up the hill, is an orange glow from the bags on the shoulders of the boys and girls cycling off to deliver the morning papers.

Day has started in Oxton Village.

Before long, a straggle of men and women will be forming outside the Post Office, some smoking roll-your-own cigarettes as they hunch against the cold. They'll gossip together, making a mist with their breath as they wait to collect their pensions and post their parcels.

The village is waking and pots of tea and toasted buns are being served in the Greenhouse room at the back of the delicatessen, known to everyone around here as the 'deli'. At the T for 2 café a few doors down from the newsagents, comes the delicious smell of eggs, bacon, sausages, beans, mushrooms and hash-brownies being prepared by Tina McDonnell. The village is humming into life. Nearly everyone is awake now and children are being dropped off at school.

Built on a ridge overlooking the rest of Birkenhead, Oxton is an extraordinary place. Once, these same rises were walked by Vikings. Not the men of popular image, raping and pillaging in horned helmets, but modest farmers and traders. The triumph is its survival as an 'oasis' in a town once famed for shipbuilding.

The classes have long mixed. When the Cammell Laird shipyard and the docks prospered in the late Victorian era, Oxton attracted the first flush of business people, and in their wake came the professionals. It wasn't quite 'top drawer', but the big houses with their luscious lawns were for families with servants, though they are not quite as grand as those built round Birkenhead Park or the rural parts of Wirral. Even so, they contrasted with the miserable streets in other parts of Birkenhead where the labouring classes dwelt.

Oxton's real growth came with the development of the industrial town. The skill of the early architects is reflected in the 37 listed buildings, a remarkable concentration in such a small community. Included are Christ Church and St Saviour's, both Anglican. Being in Birkenhead, of course, there is a large Celtic population, whose spiritual needs are met in the nearby Holy Name (Catholic) and Trinity (United Reformed) churches.

During the 1960s and '70s, the individual and defiantly middle-class nature of Oxton was threatened by the modern housing estates which spread all around. To counter this, the Oxton Society was formed in 1979; it now has 220 members. Its aims are:

To promote high standards of planning and architecture in or affecting the Oxton Conservation Area; to educate the public in the geography, history, natural history and the architecture of the area; and to secure the preservation, protection, development and improvement of features of public interest.

Wirral Borough Council formally consults the society about all planning applications concerning the developments, buildings and trees.

But the village is not inward-looking. In addition to four restaurants, two pubs, two off-licences, a Chinese takeaway, two butchers, two general stores, a chemist and charity shops, there are hairdressers, a keep-fit centre, a computer shop and a mobile phone shop. The population of the village and the conservation area is about 5000, but more than 14,000 people live in the wider ward of Oxton.

The Oxton Society's secretary is Patrick Dowling a 65-year-old retired teacher with generously-bristled eyebrows and a neat white moustache, who has lived in the village for 35 years. He is sitting in the 'deli' beneath jars of preserves, jams and pickles. "We don't have houses of mansion proportions," he says. "There are cottages and substantial villas. The village has retained its charm, though it hasn't always been easy. I have never regretted living here."

He recalls old times in the Shrewsbury Arms, affectionately known as the 'Shrew'. "You stepped off the street and you were in the lower bar, which was for the village's working men," he says. "You went up the steps and in the small front-room were the cotton-brokers, the corn merchants and the local councillors. When you went in there, there was a hush, you know, 'Who is this person?' Then there was the little snug for assignations and what have you. The licensee of the time, Ada Hanson, a formidable lady, looked after her gentlemen. She wasn't so keen on lady clients or people who asked for crisps. She didn't like greasy marks and lipstick on the glasses."

At the bottom of Rose Mount, David Adams is hanging pheasant, wild duck, pigeon, teal and partridge on the hooks outside his butcher's shop. His grandfather, George Henry Adams, a robust father of ten, began the business in 1909, passing it on to his son, Ivor. David was next. One day, his son Robert, now chopping meat in the back, will be the boss. The family bought the freehold on the present premises for £373 in 1946. This is a butcher's shop where the meat doesn't have that anaemic look favoured by supermarkets. "We sell a lot of game and venison," says David. "But we do a lot of baked products and ready meals as well these days."

Tina from T for 2 and her husband, Terry, open their café seven days a week. "We see all village life in here," she says with a knowing smile.

The day is ending and dusk is falling. Wendy Nelson is locking-up her store where you can buy brooms, gardening equipment, pet food and household goods. Soon, the restaurants will be open.

And when the moon is high over the houses of Oxton, the cats will prowl again and the people will sleep until another day begins in this timeless village.

LITTLE NESTON

The children once called the winged seed-pods of the sycamore trees whirligigs because of the way they fell to the ground. Now they are circling down on to the black earth near the old colliery, where long ago the roots of gorse spread into the slag-heaps that overlook the track, skirting the marshes to the pub. The mud out there, with the reeds spearing through the spartina grass, daily attracts the eager squelch of wellied nature-followers whose binoculars search the horizon in the hope of seeing an unexpected visitor swoop and feed.

To the urban ear, there is the flow of poetry in the words which list the birds found here: shelduck, dunlin, knot, oystercatchers, widgeon, pintail, curlew, little egret, sandpiper, greenshank, godwit, shorelark, hen harriers and peregrine falcons. The mud, when roused by your tread, looks sullen and grey, but the air smells clean and cool. The sun parts the clouds on the Clwydian hills, casting lights across the flash pools. Here, the longer-legged sea birds preen and dip.

About 200 yards along the track is the white-painted pebble dashing of the Harp Inn, where locals and travellers have slaked their thirsts for the past 221 years. You can be sure that these benches have been polished by the trousers of poachers, smugglers, jugglers, sailors, excise men, virgins and tarts, bare-knuckle fighters, fishermen, fugitives, passing preachers, singers, poets, rummies, and cribbage kings.

You'll not be disappointed when Ted Weston, in his jungle hat and camouflage jacket, strides through the pub's black door, followed by his wide-beamed border collie, Mitsy. They have walked about a quarter of a mile from their home in an old miner's cottage for his first pint of the day. He sits with his back to the window, placing the long glass on the table by his Old Holborn tin from which he pulls a few threads of rich-smelling tobacco and rolls them into a thin cigarette.

Outside, Peter Davies is looking across the marshes while Inca, his Harris Hawk, perches on a post. Such sights are not unusual at the Harp, which was built so close to the front that sandbags are still placed across the entrance to guard against the high tides of the spring and autumn.

There is a chill in the air today and the landlady, Ann Branten, is wondering when to lay the first logs of winter in the hearth. Over it, there are photographs, telling of Little Neston's past as a colliery village. One shows the last shift at the pit in 1928: Arthur Jones, Dave Parry, Joe Burkey, Joe Millington, Bill Williams, Riche Williams, John M Williams, Jack Campion, Henry Williams, and the 'cobbler' Jim Jones. They are faces from another age, each wearing a flat cap. Coal mining had been a local industry since the sixteenth century and 17 shafts were eventually sunk between Ness and Denhall. The visible slag-heaps mark the old Denhall shaft, the one closest to the pub. Thousands of men drew their wages from what became known at the Wirral Colliery.

It would be wrong to romanticise the industry from the comfort and safety of today. Early in the nineteenth century, a visitor described the Denhall mines as the most miserable and desolate place he had ever seen. Whole families, he said, went underground for a few pence a day. They lived in squalid cottages that were alive to every kind of animal and insect. The advent of steam and compulsory education led to an improvement in conditions. Although not major by national standards, the Wirral Colliery formed the culture of the local community and was responsible for the development of a dialect heard only in the Neston area. Until shortly before its closure, the mine employed up to 400 men, but with losses of about £250 week, William Davies, the owner, decided to close. Without the pumps, water soon ran into the old workings.

Many of those who came to Little Neston and its surrounds were from North Wales and they named the pub the Harp Inn. It started as three cottages built in 1750. Thirty years later, two of the cottages were converted into the pub, which retains many of the original features. The Harp has two rooms. The public bar to the left was used by the miners; their managers drank in the lounge to the right of the entrance.

Like so many places of its kind, Little Neston is now a fashionable place to live, particularly with retired couples. Modern bungalows stretch along the coast. Despite the abundance of wildlife in the marshes, some locals have also decorated the front of their homes with plaster butterflies and ladybirds. Modern dwellings with lush lawns contrast with the old colliery cottages on the rise to the village green where there stands an old-fashioned telephone kiosk, opposite the Royal Oak pub. The nearby shops are the usual mix: off-licences, general store, butcher, hairdresser and building society. Down on the shore little has changed.

Ted, who used to labour for the Water Board, has lived in the village for 38 years. "I don't go out on the marshes now," he says, "I'm too long in the tooth for that. I used to go out there shooting ducks and geese until I got caught. You couldn't get permission to shoot, so you had poach. It was all right at one time, you could go on the marsh, but then the Wildfowlers (the Dee Wildfowlers and Wetlands Management Club) took over." He didn't want to join them and gave up shooting.

"It's not really a village anymore, it is too spread out," he says. His children, Debbie and Robbie, were brought up here. "It was great for them," he recalls. "They had plenty of room to play."

In those days, the pub and its regulars were sometimes cut off by the tide. "We would be open until the early hours of the morning. The police couldn't get round here," says Ted. He breaks off for a moment to greet Peter Davies: "Hello, me old son."

Peter has entered the bar with his pointers, Sally, eight, and Milo, three. Now aged 38, Peter came to the village with his parents, Cathy and seaman Daniel, when he was a one-year-old. "I'm into fishing, shooting, hawks, ferrets," he says. "This was an adventure playground. We were out there as little kids – even on the marsh where you shouldn't go – all the dangerous places. But you have to be careful if you are inexperienced. You can easily get cut off when the tide comes in behind you."

Besides his Harris Hawk Inca, Peter has a breeding pair, Ron and Mig, who have five-week old Maya in their nest. The names Inca and Maya are taken from their homeland in Central America.

"At the beginning of October I usually start going out on the marshes. The dogs flush out rabbits, ducks, pheasants, and hopefully the hawk catches them in the local woods. The one hawk has taken two hundred and eighty-seven rabbits in one season. When she catches them, I take the rabbit off her, fetch it home to be skinned and gutted. I take the saddle and the back legs and the hawks, falcons, ferrets and dogs get the front end."

Peter holds a commercial driver's licence. He says he loves the country, but not in the same way as the armchair sentimentalists. His obvious enthusiasm for claw, tooth and blood are unsettling to those who think nature should be admired at a distance, but such people could have an important part in the future of Little Neston, which, away from the marshes, is turning into middle-class suburbia.

Before acquiring the lease to the pub, Ann Branten lectured in beauty and complementary therapy in Manchester. "It's a big change," she says with a laugh. "But everyone has been helpful and supportive. It's wonderful when I wake up in the morning, draw those curtains and look at that view, which is so panoramic – it's like being on holiday. When I first came you could see the snow on the hills in North Wales. It was really picturesque."

Lorraine Taylor is an advertising consultant, her husband, Jed is a buyer in the music industry, and they have been in Little Neston for 23 years. "I have lived in Liverpool, Surrey and London, and I can honestly say this is the friendliest area you could ever wish for," she says. "People have time for each other."

On the tracks, where men with faces blackened by coal dust once coughed in the clear light of day, bird-watchers now stand in their waxed jackets.

COSMOPOLITAN
LIVERPOOL

You can feel a pride in the different races of this city. Indeed, some feel that to be Liverpudlian is to be a member of a race apart from the rest of the country. The city is made up of many different people who come with their own customs and faiths. I wrote a series about them in 2001.

BLACK LIVERPOOL

Liverpool's part in the slave trade is well known. Here, Ray Costello, author, teacher, and lecturer, talks about how the Black community in Liverpool has been here for longer than much of the White community.

~

Ray Costello tells the story of how a white mother and her daughter stood on some coffee-house steps in the 1770s, watching a black girl being separated from her mother. The little white girl became very distressed. "Don't worry, dear, it's like when Flossy lost her pups," said her mother, in a comforting tone.

"She wasn't an evil woman," Ray said. "That's the way it was. But her daughter just saw another little girl who was very unhappy."

In his pale blue cardigan, slacks and white shirt, Ray Costello looks like the sort of chap you might see buttering crumpets in a seaside café, or enjoying the sun on the local golf links. He smiles at this comfortable image. After all, his family has been here long enough to pick up some of the native customs. Then he laughs in a long, rumbling tone that suggests a pride and confidence in the man he feels himself to be.

Whatever others may think, he's a Liverpool black, a descendent of the almost forgotten community that settled in the city during the mid-eighteenth and early nineteenth centuries. Down the family tree, there has been some mixing with white people, which went far beyond holding hands and singing hymns, and they left their mark too. But it is the blood of his black forebears that he feels pumping through his veins.

This is true of all national or racial minorities. The Scotsman whose relatives have been jellying eels since Bow bells first clanged, still strides to the rugby match against the 'auld enemy' in his kilt and sporran. But for Ray's people, it is more serious. They want their fellow citizens to know that they were here when Liverpool was a small fishing port, long before the mass emigrations from mainland Europe and Ireland.

"One of the things that I have learnt is that the black presence has been here since at least seventeen thirty, but I hope someone will push the boundaries back even further than that," he said at his smart, modern house in Aigburth. "The black community in Liverpool really took off after the American War of Independence. King George III offered freedom to every black slave who had remained loyal to Britain. They fled their rebel owners and were formed into black regiments with British officers. Others were scouts. Some were spies. One black looked the same as another black to an American slave owner.

"When Britain lost America, they were shipped off to London via Liverpool, so the city was full of blacks in regimental colours. Many of these were shipped off to Africa to found the colony in Sierra Leone." Its present capital, Freetown, became a sanctuary for former slaves in 1787, before the country was made a British colony in 1808.

"To this day, the names in Sierra Leone are the same as those in Liverpool and, to some extent, America," said Ray. "These, of course, were slave names like Charles and Cole. The blacks did exactly the same as the Irish who had hoped to go to America. They ran out of money and settled in Liverpool where there was already a small black community.

"People didn't have the same preconceptions then. They might have been wary of blacks because they looked different. They would have been frighteningly strange people. But the feeling that black people were inferior wasn't there so much. That came with slavery and was intensified by the colonial period in the later part of the nineteenth century. The important point is that black people were being born in Liverpool from the seventeen seventies, maybe earlier."

Some were servants in the big houses. Many became seamen. Others ran small businesses, or survived in any way they could. Ironically, a few were captured by gangs and taken to America. Ray said, "We have accounts of Liverpool blacks being kidnapped as early as 1810 and sold as slaves in Charleston." However, the normal pattern was for ships to leave Liverpool with trading goods like guns, trinkets, utensils and cloths. These would be taken to the coast of West Africa where the slaves would be collected and delivered to plantations in America and the West Indies.

Although the movement against slavery was gathering momentum in this country by the end of the eighteenth century, there was a fashion in rich society for keeping young black people, with the boys dressed in turbans and spangles, like Indian princes.

"The trouble was that in time they would get five o'clock shadow or start being cheeky," Ray said. "Then they would be thrown out on the streets, ending up as part of the Liverpool black population, rummaging with everyone else.

"Sometimes the poor whites were very good allies of the Liverpool blacks. A Portuguese captain tried to tempt some blacks on board his ship, saying that there was a seafaring job, when he really wanted to sell them at Charleston. He wanted to keep them in the local bridewell (police cells). But the poor whites stormed the building demanding their release."

There were examples of white people sharing accommodation with black people. Sometimes friendships resulted in marriage. In many families, however, this was taboo and resulted in one partner or the other being ex-communicated. Ray punctuates many of his observations with laughter. He speaks of what were once called 'half-caste' children. "Dual heritage is the politically correct term," he said. "But you have to do more than change words."

Does Ray think his blood is black, white, or just red like everyone else? "Oh, I haven't totted it up," he answers with another booming laugh. "But I would identify myself entirely with the blacks because it is a mixed race community, even though I am not a quarter, or even an eighth black.

"The common factor which keeps the black community united is racism. In the street, white people didn't say, 'That fine fellow seems to be one quarter black and therefore a bit better than all black'. They just said he was black. You see, this is what the Somalis haven't got yet. They don't say this fellow is from the proud Somali nation – they just say, 'He's another black'. That what it's about.

"Since the nineteen fifties in Liverpool there has been a very strong sense of racial togetherness. People have realised that the only way you get anywhere is by keeping that spirit."

It was an old community, which had survived by drawing in different cultures. In exactly the same way as people may claim to be Irish or Welsh, despite inter-marrying with the English, his people chose their own identity. Although it's an obvious point, black people look different. This has led to a prejudice not suffered by Liverpudlians from the many other nations – Scandinavians, the French Huguenots, the Irish etc. Among the poorer communities, a pecking order developed, which generally disadvantaged black people.

It would be wrong to think of Liverpool 8 as a ghetto. At least as many black people live in other parts of Merseyside. A lot of the older white Liverpool families have some black ancestry, Ray explained.

"I love Liverpool. My roots are in this city. I think that people have just got to realise that the black population is not only here to stay, but has been here longer than half of the white population. It is the fascinating story of an invisible people."

Ray's own line can be traced back to shoemaker Francis James, the son of a Scotsman who married a black woman in Hamilton, Bermuda. Their son, Edward, came to Liverpool in the 1850s and married Harriet Gates of Barnton, Cheshire, a Methodist who became a Quaker, a faith that practised racial tolerance. Edward was a sailor who was in port often enough to provide his wife with seven children – Edward, Moira, Albert (Ray's grandfather), Edith, Florence, William and Agnes. Another child died in infancy.

Edward's hard-working wife, Harriet, ran a grocery store in Wellington Road, Dingle. At 3am each day she rose to bake the cakes, and by 5am, as the city awoke, she would be ladling milk from great churns into jugs. When her son was 13, Edward, a dapper fellow, began helping in the shop and received a small wage.

One night in the 1890s, young Edward decided to see how the other half lived and ordered a slap-up meal in a swanky restaurant. A few days later, he was dead after suffering the agonies of food poisoning. The family was heartbroken to see their ambitious boy taken away from them. The restaurant wasn't prosecuted.

One of their other sons, Albert, who would become Ray's grandfather, was a junior librarian when he enlisted the Royal Field Artillery Regiment in 1914. He later became an iron moulder. Albert married Ethel Vernon Jones, a white woman from Jersey. They had Ray's mother, Edith, now in her 80s. Edith married a white RAF man called Francis Costello and Ray was their only child.

The young Ray and his mother Edith moved to Selbourne Street, Toxteth, into the terraced home of his great auntie Agnes and her husband Henry Brew, a Ghanaian seaman. Ray commented, "Throughout all this, the black part of me had been diluting," but the family's essentially black ancestry can be seen in a photograph of Edward James' great-great-grandchildren, 12-year-old Soraya and 17-year-old Gemma.

Ray was educated at Granby Street School and the CF Mott teachers' training college. He taught at Windsor Street School and Harrington County Primary and then became a special needs teacher in Speke primary schools. He was awarded a Masters degree in Education in 1980 and was the first person from the old black community to be awarded a PhD in education from Liverpool University. Now retired from teaching, Ray is an independent education adviser and give talks on the under-achievement of children of Afro/Caribbean descent to teachers and community groups.

KEY DATES

1730s-40s: Small numbers of blacks from West Africa come to Liverpool as sailors and house servants. A few, usually the sons of daughters of tribal leaders, are educated in the city.

1775: Skirmishes at Lexington and Concord begin the American Revolution. Black slaves who remain loyal to Britain are promised their freedom. Some come to Britain and settle in ports including Liverpool and London.

1779-92: Log of the Slave Trade Boom in Liverpool covers this period. Slavery was important to the economy of colonial powers such as Spain, Portugal and Britain throughout the sixteenth, seventeenth and eighteenth centuries.

1788: William Wilberforce, Granville Sharp and Thomas Clarkson, supported by Quakers, start pressing for the abolition of the slave trade.

1807: Slavery abolished in Britain.

1833: Slavery abolished in the British Empire.

1863: Emancipation Proclamation in the USA leads the way for the abolition of slavery after Union forces defeat on the Confederacy in 1865.

Late nineteenth century: Colonial expansion in Africa by Britain, France and other European countries reinforces the notion of white superiority.

1981: Riots in Toxteth as angry black people protest against their status as 'second-class citizens'.

1991: Census shows that there were 2,487 black African, 1,495 black Caribbean and 3,265 black people of other origin in the city.

2001: Census shows that there were 3,071 black African, 1,083 Caribbean and 1,223 other black people.

THE CHINESE COMMUNITY

Liverpool has Britain's oldest Chinatown. It attracts people of all nationalities for its Chinese New Year celebrations, and it boasts some of the finest Chinese restaurants and a magnificent new archway. In this piece, we meet some of the regulars at the Merseyside Chinese Community Association and learn about the great traditions that continue to hold the community together.

~

When she smiles, Wai Mui Chan's lips almost touch her ear lobes which have been stretched by jewellery and the passing of years. To her people, such lobes are a symbol of a long stay on earth; their length is her dignity. This is the face of a fine old lady of 92, and you can see the faint trace of purple veins running down her temples. The smile is wonderful and you think that it should be kept forever, but Wai Mui doesn't think like that at all. She smiles for the friend she's with, or as a greeting to a stranger. For her, a smile is a private thing, just from one person to the other. It's not there for everyone to stare at, so she won't agree to it being photographed. Westerners may think it's a good thing for people to have their shadows transferred to paper, but she doesn't. They didn't do that in Tapmum, where she was raised.

Wai Mui Chan is in the dining-room run by the Merseyside Chinese Community Association (MCCA) in Great George's Square, Liverpool. The centre's supervisor, Jimmy Hui, sits close and whispers to her, trying to persuade her to have the picture taken. But it's to no avail. "If you tell an old Chinese woman how lovely she looks, she'll deny it," says Jimmy. "They're very traditional people."

Wai Mui trusts Jimmy, although they are from different generations. A few weeks ago, the tiny lady – not more than 4ft 8in in height and even less than that when bent over her walking stick – stumbled off the minibus that takes her and some friends from the dining-room to their home in sheltered accommodation in Upper Parliament Street. It wasn't a bad fall, but she grazed her finger and

Jimmy carefully took her hand, which is swollen with arthritis and has veins that stand out under a pale layer of skin, and applied a plaster to it. Wai Mui was so grateful that she gave Jimmy a tiny red envelope decorated in gold. Inside, she had folded a fiver. Out of modesty, she told him it was empty – this was a custom she understood. It wasn't the money that counted; it was an expression of thanks from an old lady. Even so, she wouldn't be photographed for posterity, she said, smiling behind her oval glasses.

This little story tells a lot about the Chinese culture that still thrives in Liverpool amongst the old and the young. There are four words that remind these people of how it used to be, and should be still. The words don't translate easily into English, but they are 'lai' – politeness, manners, diffidence, 'yea' – a sense of honesty, duty or obligation to your fellow humans, 'lim' an incorruptible morality, and 'chee' – dignity, avoiding shame. This is the wisdom of Confucius.

Chinese sailors began settling in Liverpool in the middle of the nineteenth century. The Blue Funnel Line, founded in 1865, was the first to have a direct steamship link between Britain and China. Only two Chinese 'boys' were included among the 700 people it employed between 1871-1873. In 1881, the official census recorded 15 Chinese-born residents in Liverpool and Birkenhead. The resident population has fluctuated over the years, but it has never exceeded 8,000. It has never been a large community, though it is the oldest in the UK. The 1991 census showed 3,337 Chinese living in Liverpool.

Liverpool was part of the general Chinese diaspora. The early immigrants settled in a district between Cleveland Square, Pitt Street and Frederick Street. It was a humming, poor neighbourhood, where the quiet, shy Chinese, often pigtailed and dressed in strange, baggy smocks, found themselves outnumbered by the Scandinavians, European Jews and Africans. Most were bachelors. Some married local girls. Many remained single. Population growth was slow. This was not a large, steaming Chinatown closed to the outside world like those growing in the American seaports.

World War I brought a rapid rise in Liverpool's Chinese community. A report in 1918, compiled by the Ministry of Shipping on the supply of seamen, listed 3,200 Chinese men on shore, of whom 2,850 were associated with shipping.

While most were travellers, there was, by early last century, the embryo of a more settled community. Included in it were Chow Ghee, who ran a boarding house, Ko Foo Kee the chandler, Chow Too Kee the huckster, Emily Ah Foo the Chinese agent, Chong On the tailor and Kwok Fong the private detective. These Chinese people generally came from Guandong Province and Hong Kong.

Boarding-houses and laundries were popular businesses because the whole family could be involved. At one time, more than a quarter of Liverpool's Chinese population was employed in laundries. These were often run from terraced houses, with the washing facilities under a corrugated room in the backyard. The 'shop', with an ironing board, would be in the front parlour. Drying was carried out in the back room.

During the 1930s, the Merseyside Chinese community dropped in number to some 530 and that included British-born wives. The war was to change that pattern of decline temporarily. Liverpool was the headquarters of the Western Approaches and home of the Chinese Merchant Seamen's Pool, which included some 15,000 men, many from Shanghai and other parts of the Chinese mainland. However, as was the case after World War I, the population quickly dispersed.

The economic boom of the 1950s led to a gradual increase in population. In 1955 there were estimated to be 1,000 Chinese in Liverpool. At this time, restaurants began replacing laundries as the economic mainstay of the community. Eating at these restaurants, which later developed the trademark style of flock wallpaper and giant goldfish tanks, became popular with Britons who would soak up their beer on Friday and Saturday nights with curry and rice. Three-course business lunches that undercut the local opposition brought Chinese meals to the attention of a wider public. However, the possibilities of Chinese food had been appreciated in certain circles 20 years before that.

For just two old pence, Foo Nam Low's place in Pitt Street served ham bows. For a few pence more you could have chicken wings or legs. A jug of chop suey was a bob (5p). A favourite with the locals was rice juk – boiled rice with stock, dung choi (Chinese cabbage) and meat. An egg and whole spring onions would be added. Among the early eating-houses was Frank's English 'chippy', where the mushy peas soaked the newspaper wrapping until it was green. In a cultural exchange, many Chinese children would spend their pennies there, much to the disapproval of the traditional elders.

The present Chinatown in the Nelson Street area of the city grew on the back of the restaurant boom, but it is also a shopping area with several modern housing developments. It is quite open, but 'they keep themselves to themselves' is an expression much used to describe the community.

The Pagoda in Henry Street is used as an independent educational, training, cultural, social and administrative headquarters. The MCCA is funded by Liverpool City Council and produces *Silk Road News*, a bilingual 12-page newspaper which appears six times a year and organises a carers' network for old people. These old people meet at the association's dining-room in Great George's Square during the week for a £1.50 meal that is designed to be nutritious and uses standard Chinese ingredients like vegetables, spare ribs, black bean sauce, pork stock and bean curd, with various dishes spiced with garlic. The chop-sticks symbolise their tolerant manner, the notion of everyone eating from the table, sharing from the same dishes. The building is rented from the Chinese Gospel Church.

Jimmy is the supervisor of the MCCA. He is married to Margaret, his childhood sweetheart from Hong Kong. They have raised three children in England, Hayley and Julie, both medical students, and Andrew, a business student. A few yards from Jimmy, the old ladies play Hakka, a traditional card game. Some reluctantly agree to be photographed. There is a newcomer with them today, Jenny Tan who is 14 and studying maths, English and French at the St George of England High School, Bootle.

"The new generation respects the older people. In that way the families stay together," says Jimmy Hui. "It is the wisdom of the ages."

With that wisdom, the Chinese have quietly gone about their business.

KEY DATES

551-479 BC: Life of Confucius, the great moral teacher, whose ideas are still followed by some Liverpool Chinese.

1839-42: First Opium War. Chinese officials tried to prevent the importation of opium. Opium from India paid for Britain's importation of goods from China. Defeat results in China opening its ports, including Hong Kong.

1850s: Chinese sailors arrive on Merseyside.

1856-60: Second Opium War. Britain and France crush Chinese resistance to the trade.

1865: Blue Funnel Line opens a steamship link between Britain and China.

1899: Britain acquires Hong Kong on a 99-year lease.

1900: Anti-Western Boxer Rebellion defeated by an alliance of powers.

1914-18: World War I leads to an increase in the Liverpool Chinese community.

1940s: Liverpool becomes headquarters of the Western Approaches. Chinese Merchant Seamen's Pool estimated at 15,000. Post-war: Chinese population falls.

1950s: Popularity of Chinese food leads to proliferation of restaurants and takeaways.

1989: More than 2000 killed after pro-democracy demonstrations in Tianamen Square.

1997: Hong Kong returned to China.

THE JEWISH COMMUNITY

Joseph Wolfman, archivist to the Merseyside Jewish Representative Council, explains how the Jews first came to Liverpool, established their community and came to offer the city so much.

~

The old man in the skullcap stares from the electric candles and the shining chandeliers to the arches and columns that support this place of rich and vivid colours where his people worship their God. Joseph Wolfman sighs before resting the arm of his weathered jacket on the end of a pew. It all seems a lot of fuss to him. He even had to take off his old raincoat to look smart for the photograph and it's very cold in here. Next, they'll ask him to wear a tie! The 82-year-old grandfather is evidently not a man who overly bothers about outward appearances. But when tourists first step through the mighty oak doors into the full glory of the building, they often whisper 'Jesus Christ' and whistle in wonder at the splendour of everything around them. The Jews, who have seen it all before, laugh at their guests' temporary loss of decorum.

It wasn't always like this, as Mr Wolfman knows. He is the unpaid archivist to the Merseyside Jewish Representative Council. The first Jews in Liverpool formed their congregation in a modest cottage, just off Stanley Street. It was owned by Joseph Clegg, Liverpool's mayor in 1748. Local people called it the 'Jews' synagogue', as though there was another kind of synagogue, and the land where it stood was called Synagogue Court on the old maps. It is listed in the *Liverpool Memorandum Book* of 1753, taking its place after ten churches and chapels. With the burial ground around it, the site occupied 26 yards on the east and west, 14 yards on the north and nine-and-a-half yards on the south.

Although the big Russian pogroms did not begin until the 1880s, anti-Semitism had been rife in Europe for centuries. In many towns and cities, the Jews were compelled to live in ghettos as a result of a papal edict in 1555. By contrast, England was a free society where they were able to practise their religion and customs without fear of repression. In Germany, which was then divided into small states, the treatment of Jews depended on the local rulers. "But they could be quite severe," said Mr Wolfman. "They would have to live in ghettos and be in the ghettos by a certain time at night. In Prussia, only the eldest son could marry. You couldn't indulge in any trade where the Christian guilds were prominent. In England the only real restriction was joining the army because you had to take a Christian oath."

Ports appealed to Jews, and Portsmouth became their biggest settlement outside London. The growth of Liverpool in the eighteenth century was another attraction. In the bustle of commerce and the hum of foreign tongues, strangers didn't stand out.

"The Jews sold goods to sailors, mainly what they called slops (ready-made clothing, like loose-fitting trousers) and jewellery: necklaces and earrings, and knives and razors with costly handles," said Mr Wolfman. "I have this theory, and it is only a theory, that a synagogue was established here because of the trade between Liverpool and the West Indies, where there was a settled and quite rich Jewish community who could send ships to Liverpool and supervise cargoes. They would have had enough money and know-how to do that."

How did he visualise these people? "Some of the pedlars and hawkers moving around the country would have worn outlandish clothes," he said. "These would be the poor Jews, unsettled, wandering about. But those who had settled here would wear typical working men's dress, like the host people."

Despite their tough beginnings in the city, a small bourgeois element gradually developed in the Jewish community, allowing for a sense of permanence not found in other towns. "No other place in the north of England had a settled place of worship. Manchester did have somewhere, probably a stockroom, but it only lasted for about ten years."

In the absence of custom-built synagogues, the Jews tended to gather in converted houses. They worshipped in the cottage for about 20 years, before transferring to a stockroom in Turton Court, down by the docks. "They probably couldn't afford the rent to stay in Synagogue Court," said Mr Wolfman. There was a strong suspicion that the amount expected from the Jews exceeded the true value of the building.

The move also meant that they had lost their cemetery. While they were in Turton Court, they bought a plot of land in Frederick Street where they also acquired a house, which opened as a synagogue in 1778. About 50 people could worship in the upstairs rooms. Downstairs, they had the ritual bath or 'mikveh' used to 'cleanse' women when they were menstruating. The mikveh had to have running water, so, in addition to its religious significance, it was a forerunner of the public wash-house opened in Upper Frederick Street in 1842 by Kitty Wilkinson, the celebrated friend of the poor.

Around this time, the Jewish population was small but growing with the port. At the start of the nineteenth century, Liverpool's population was 78,000 and the hard-working merchant class of Jews was becoming increasingly influential. In 1804, they took the bold step of hiring an architect to design a synagogue befitting of their status. The man chosen was John Harrison, pupil and nephew of Thomas Harrison, famed designer of the Lyceum on Bold Street. John matched his uncle with the Grecian-fronted synagogue in Seel Street. The synagogue held some 300 people and was consecrated in 1807. This was very much the place of the prosperous Jews who were more Anglicised in their taste and manners.

Then a schism opened. A breakaway faction called themselves the New Hebrew Congregation and they moved into premises at the corner of Hardman Street and Pilgrim Street. Both groups were recognised by the Chief Rabbi. The new sect decided they should have an architecturally-designed synagogue. This commission was given to Thomas Wylie. His synagogue in Hope Place was consecrated in 1857. It is now the Unity Theatre.

Not to be outdone, the Old Hebrew Congregation in 1868 proposed what was to become one of the grandest buildings in Liverpool – their synagogue on Princes Road, Toxteth, erected on land offered by Lord Sefton on very reasonable terms. The executive committee was determined that it should be worthy of the "great town of Liverpool" (Liverpool didn't become a city until 1880).

The status of Jews in Britain had now improved, though anti-Semitism was still prevalent in certain classes. They were not officially allowed to be members of Parliament, or take municipal office until 1858. Benjamin Disraeli (Prime Minister 1874-80), who had been elected into Parliament in 1837 was baptised as a Christian. In Liverpool, Charles Mozley became the first Jewish mayor in 1863. Soon, the people, who were to play such a prominent part in the commerce and professional life of Merseyside, would be able to praise God in some opulence and style.

After a competition, the design of the building was entrusted to William and George Audsley who decided on "an eclectic mixture of the best of the eastern and western schools of art". The foundation stone was laid on 23 December 1872, and the building, with seats for 350 women and 450 men, was consecrated by the Chief Rabbi on 3 September 1874. The total cost was £15,000.

With the waves of anti-Semitism that culminated in the Russian and Polish pogroms of the 1880s, Liverpool's Jewish population increased to about 3,000. This increase resulted in some cultural tension between the assimilated Jewish community and the strangers. "They came, looked at the synagogue, and wondered why they were in an English cathedral," said Mr Wolfman. "They stepped inside and found it far too English, too stiff upper lip. They were used to something more like a Baptist church for black people, with that sort of fervour."

Joseph Wolfman was the son of Samuel and Sophia Wolfman. The family lived above the drapery shop run by his father in County Road, Walton. By his earlier marriage to Pearl, Samuel had two sons, Jacob and Abraham, and a daughter, Minnie.

"Minnie married Alfred Urding, who was a councillor in the Conservative interest, representing Netherfield which was strongly Orange," said Mr Wolfman. "We used to joke about how there was the good Jew leading the extreme Protestant processions."

Mr Wolfman is now a member of the progressive synagogue in Church Road, Wavertree. As a child, he attended the Arnot Street primary school in Walton. From there he went to Liverpool Collegiate and then to Wadham College Oxford, where he studied classics. For more than 30 years he taught English at Oldershaw School, Wallasey. He has been married to Sonia for more than 50 years and they have four children, Selma, Matthew, Jonathan and Vanessa, who all live in Kent.

Although it is a small community of about 3000, many of whom are elderly, the Jews have made a huge contribution to the well-being of Merseyside. It is impossible to name all their distinguished men and women here, but a list would include: David Lewis, founder of Lewis's Department Stores; Alderman Louis Cohen, chairman of Lewis's who became Lord Mayor of Liverpool in 1899; Lord Herbert Samuel, the first High Commissioner for Palestine (1920-25) and the first Jew to enter the Cabinet; the solicitors Harry Livermore and Rex

Makin; Cecil Moss, the eminent gynaecologist who escorts parties around the Princes Road synagogue; Edwina Currie, the former Conservative minister, author, journalist and broadcaster; and, of course Frankie Vaughan (Abelson), the high-kicking boy from Toxteth in the silk topper, who offered the girls moonlight and romance.

KEY DATES

1066: Jews come to England following the Norman Conquest.

1291: Jews expelled following an edict from Edward I.

1673: Jews granted religious liberties by Charles II.

1740s: Beginning of Jewish community in Liverpool.

1753: Synagogue recorded off Stanley Street, Liverpool.

1770s: Stockroom in Turton Court on the docks used as a synagogue.

1778: Synagogue for 50 worshippers open in Frederick Street, Liverpool.

1807: Synagogue for about 300 people consecrated in Seel Street, Liverpool.

1842: Split in the Seel Street congregation. The Old Hebrew Congregation stays.

1842: New Hebrew Congregation moves into premises on Hardman Street / Pilgrim Street, Liverpool.

1857: New Hebrew Congregation synagogue consecrated in Hope Place, Liverpool.

1858: Jews permitted to stand for Parliament or take municipal office.

1868: Old Jewish Congregation proposes synagogue in Princes Road, Liverpool.

1872: Foundation stone laid in Princes Road synagogue.

1874: It opens among much pomp.

1879: Princes Road synagogue has to be treated for dry rot.

1940-42: Princes Road synagogue suffers war damage.

1948: More dry rot at Princes Road.

1978: Fire destroys the Ark in Princes Road.

1997: The Princes Road synagogue's listing is raised to Grade II.

THE SOMALI COMMUNITY

They came here to escape life in one of the world's most turbulent countries, riven first by the colonial ambitions of European powers and then by the ceaseless feuding of its own nomadic clans.

~

At first, strangers may wonder whether the vivid orange colour of the grizzled whiskers on some of the old men holds some deep religious significance, but it is just common vanity. Like the rest of us, the Somali men try to keep in check the creeping of the years by dying their greying hair. The colour is from the juice of henna leaves.

They are sitting on meeting-hall-style chairs and wooden benches in a downstairs room with a high ceiling in their house at the end of Granby Street. It's an area where many of the shops are shuttered and litter lies in the gardens of abandoned homes. Once, outsiders called it 'Little Harlem' because it was home to people from so many races. Now, everyone knows it as Toxteth.

Above the front door of the house is a sign saying 'Merseyside Somali Community', written on red, white and green horizontal stripes with a black star in the middle. "Is that your flag?" I ask a young man, believing it to be a simple question. He pauses for some seconds as the cars pass, and then he looks up to the sleeting sky and shakes his head. "That's a complicated question," he says. It is, in fact, the flag for the northern region. The national flag is actually blue with a white star in the middle, with each of its tips representing a region.

In fact, everything about Somalia is complicated, but they are a wonderful people with a magical talent for making a fork from every straight line. Some of the confusion in their lives can be seen in the room where they meet and smoke cigarettes – the old men in baggy, short-legged trousers with freshly-laundered 'koofiyads' or caps, reaching down the generations to the rapidly westernised young men in their leather jackets, jeans and bare heads. The incessant chatter of a strange tongue rises with the steam from mugs of dark brown tea.

Somalia didn't have a written language until 1972, which means that the people, particularly the older ones, rely on a rich oral tradition of story-telling. Good talkers have a special place in the community, remembering the poems that marked the progress of the people. These poems can be long pieces as they were devised for a nomadic people unhurried by the steps of time. In modern societies where almost everything is governed by the clock, some of the charm of these customs is lost.

Although nominally a nation, the Somalis cling to the ways of their forebears whose primary loyalty was to the clan. This may explain why, what seems a simple request to the western mind, provokes animated discussion punctuated by expressive gestures amongst the Somalis. For example, securing permission to photograph the group gathered in Granby Street opened a debate which ended with some agreeing and others refusing.

The Somalis didn't start settling in Liverpool until the 1880s when small numbers joined the British Merchant Navy. A small number of sons from affluent families also came here to be educated at the beginning of the last century, before returning home with all sorts of new ideas. Generally, the Somalis were seen as part of the wider black community in Toxteth, without having a particular identity.

That was to change in the 1970s when war broke out with Ethiopia about the disputed Ogaden Desert, resulting in more than one million refugees, mostly nomads, fleeing to Somalia. Since then, war, drought and famine have followed each other in a deadly cycle, greatly adding to the misery of an already impoverished country. Understandably, many sought a better life elsewhere.

Historically, the region stirred the colonial ambitions of Italy, Britain and France, with the largest area becoming part of Italian East Africa in 1936. In 1960, the Italian area, held after World War II as a UN protectorate, joined with British Somaliland to become the United Republic of Somaliland. It is estimated that about 5000 Somalis, all Muslims, now reside in Liverpool. For many of them, this has meant huge cultural changes.

Ahmed Aideed is the deputy manager of the Liverpool Muslim Society, the Al Rahma Day Centre. At 32, he is one of the new generation of Somalis, keenly aware of the difficulties faced by an Islamic people of the desert who speak hardly any English and have to adjust to life in a commercially-driven and largely secular country. Sitting opposite is his half-brother Essa Awad Egeh, the chairman of the centre.

"There is very little recorded history of the Somalis in Liverpool," said Ahmed. "If you go to the libraries or the museums, you won't see any photographs or anything like that. The earliest Somalis in Liverpool were seamen on Merchant Navy ships. The majority of the current population came here during the civil war of the nineteen eighties. The Somali elders who were here applied for visas for their families.

"Basically, there are three groups of Somalis. We have the older generation, of whom there are fewer and fewer. Many of them died and some returned to Somalia. Then we had those who came around the more recent troubles. For instance, I came in nineteen eighty-six. My brother (Essa Awad Egeh) has been here for more than forty years. Finally, we have the new arrivals. Most come on visas. You may find that some are asylum seekers."

They have four community centres – two for the men in Granby and the women's groups, which run a wide variety of courses and meet at Beaconsfield Street and Lodge Lane. "The women are happy to meet on their own," said Ahmed. "One of the interesting things I have found in western societies is that if you have one woman among a group of men, she may suffer sexual harassment. But if you brought the most wicked group of Somali men together and you put one woman in the middle of them, they would all become shy."

"The Somalis are traditionally nomads," Ahmed said. "They will never, ever settle in one place. That affects their esteem in modern societies. These families went back to Somalia. Between the nineteen fifties and the civil war their numbers here dwindled."

Ahmed believed that the nomadic spirit of the people was still strong. "It is amazing to say, but somehow the seed of nomadic life is still with us. I don't particularly like travelling, but the desire to move from city to city stems from our culture." Essa added that both his father and grandfather had been seafarers.

For the new generation, unemployment was the main problem, said Ahmed. Some of them found solace in chewing leaves from the khat shrub. It is shipped here from Kenya and sold legally in bunches at prices which vary according to supply.

"That has caused a great deal of trouble among the community," he said. "It looks like the coca plant and it is chewed by people in Somali, Yemen, and Kenya, where the leaves are more potent. It is legal in Britain and Holland. In America, it is classified as a hard drug. It causes psychosis and paranoia. There have been four suicides in Liverpool over the past five years that could be attributed to the drug. If you do it moderately, once or twice a week, it might not do much harm. But if you chew it all night, to escape from the problems of unemployment, it keeps you awake."

Another problem for the young was the looser discipline in western society. "Traditionally, in Somali communities, the father has control of the kids. When they came here they found that that was not the case," said Ahmed. "You cannot slap your child, you know, that sort of thing. Also, there have been too many drop-outs among the Somali children in schools. You see too many Somali kids congregating on street corners. That is causing friction and dividing the community between the old, who hold the traditional ways, and some of the young ones, whom you could categorise as delinquent."

He felt that a solution to these problems would be a single, Somali community centre, where all the youth could meet. It was a familiar story. The faith of the fathers was being weakened by the temptations of modern western culture, such as TV, pop music and fashion.

Ayan Jama is just 12 years old. Her family fled the violence that began in 1991 and walked 800 miles to Ethiopia. That war resulted in some 50,000 people being killed. She was born just over the Ethiopian border. The family then left Africa for Liverpool, where they had relatives. "I have lots of English friends, but I am a Somali, and one day I want to visit," she said. So young Ayan, who speaks English, is now learning Somali.

KEY DATES

700: Islam established by Arab traders in coastal regions of what is now Somalia.

900: Mogadishu (the present capital) is founded as a trading centre.

1887: Britain establishes the protectorate of Somaliland in the north. Somali seamen begin settling in Liverpool.

1896: France founds a small colony in what is now Djibouti.

1889: Italy occupies the central region and begins pushing south.

1936: Fascist Italy joins Italian Somaliland with Somali regions of East Africa to form Italian East Africa.

1940: Italy invades British Somaliland.

1941: Britain regains lost territory and captures the Italian colony.

1950: Italy regains its colony as a UN trust.

1950s: Small numbers of Somalis settle in Liverpool.

1960: Both Somalilands are granted independence.

1969: The army led by Soad Barre forms an Islamic republic.

1970s: War with Ethiopia over control of the Ogaden Desert. Some Somalis flee to relatives in Liverpool.

1980: Liverpool Somali community grows as chaos continues in their homeland.

1991: Barre overthrown by the United Somali Congress, but country sinks into bloody civil war followed by drought and famine.

1992: After much delay and confusion, a UN-approved, US-led task force begins distributing aid. In 1993, it is replaced by 28,000-strong UN force. Between June and November, 2000 Somalis and 90 UN troops are killed in skirmishes.

1994: Western troops pull out, leaving Indian, Pakistani and Egyptian soldiers who are driven out.

1995: All UN troops withdraw, as political chaos continues.

1997: 26 out of 28 factions agree on a 13-member Presidential Council and a 189-member Council of Deputies in preparation for elections not later than **2003.** Fierce fighting breaks out. Throughout the 1990s, Somalis seek refuge in Liverpool, as troubles continue at home.

THE GERMAN COMMUNITY

People from the Liverpool Deutsche Kirche reflect on the challenges faced by their community and how it looks to the future.

~

There is a moment every year when this little congregation is filled by a yearning for another place. It comes late on Christmas Eve when they sit on the floral, cushioned, wooden chairs that are lined in rows of five, beneath the red and green glass baubles hanging from branches of fir. At the back of the brick chapel, the organist presses the keys and the people rise to sing *Stille Nacht*.

To most of us, it is a lovely carol. To the German community in Liverpool, it is the melody of home, rolling back, through poetic verse, to the green memories of childhood. This is the time, perhaps the only time, when they do feel apart, for a German Christmas is different. *Silent Night* is not the same as *Stille Nacht*.

Even their pastor, Martin Gunter, whose English flows with ease, says there is something in the German sentiment which cannot be translated because the words carry their own mood. He is in discussion with his friends from the Deutsche Kirche who have gathered for coffee and fruitcake. Almost hidden by trees, the hall, which is attached to the church, was built in 1959 on the corner of the fading Regency glamour of Canning Street and Bedford Street. Under them is the rubble of the earlier German Church, a grand edifice with a prominent steeple severely damaged during the Luftwaffe's bombing raids on the Mersey docks. The irony is not lost on the group around the table. There is much shrugging of shoulders and shaking of heads, even a little laughter – these things happen in war, they say.

It was difficult being a German in the city during both world wars when a foreign-sounding name was in itself sufficient to stir the anger of the local people who once had been your friends. Some were repatriated to Germany, others were held in internment camps. When they returned to the ruins of their church, only the vestry was still standing. With determination and faith, they began forming a new congregation in a Protestant tradition, combining Lutherans, Unitarians and other sects.

They meet for services on the second and fourth Sundays of every month. It is comforting for them to speak and sing in the mother tongue. Their numbers are falling – Germans marry Britons, then the children go their own way. So, baptisms are important. At the end of the table, Annette is nursing her baby, Maja. Sighs from this sleeping child sound the future of the Germans in Liverpool.

Annette came here in September 1997 to train in midwifery at the Women's Hospital. Then she met and fell in love with William Byrne. When they married, they took the name Grams-Byrne, and one nation reached out to another in the spirit of love. Six months ago, Maja was born. "My husband is a Catholic," Annette said, "and Maja will be brought up knowing about several religions, so that she is open-minded. But she will be baptised here and come with me to this church."

Hermine Hodgins, a retired teacher, was raised in Stuttgart. She is married to Desmond, who teaches German. They have two grown-up sons: Ralph, who lives in Bebington, and William, who works in the European patents office in Munich. For almost 40 years, Hermine has watched the development of the German community on Merseyside, making her their unofficial historian. But could she imagine the early families stepping ashore here with their bundles of belongings, bewildered – their legs still wobbling to the motion of the sea – as they searched the faces of strangers for a smile?

"A lot of German people who wanted to go on to America got stuck in Liverpool because their money ran out," she said. "They were hardy people and would sleep for several nights on the Pier Head. But missionaries would pick them up and offer them shelter. They were very poor in the beginning and used to live in the Scotland Road area."

These early settlers came from the various Germanic states that were drawn into a single nation by Otto Bismark in 1871. In the middle of the nineteenth century, life was tough in the homeland. "It was very insecure in those days," said Hermine. "The economic welfare was dreadful. The young people would seek their fortune somewhere else. They would get on with life, just as the immigrants do nowadays."

Liverpool's population was increasing at an alarming rate. In 1821, the trickle of Germans merged into a population of 119,000. In 1841, that population had increased to 286,000, and by 1861 it had reached 444,000. Hunger, disease and death haunted the dank cellars, particularly after the Irish potato famine. Undoubtedly, some Germans were sucked into this misery, but others began to establish themselves.

In 1845, Dr Joseph Baylee, an Anglican and head of St Aidan's Theological College, Birkenhead, had founded the Mission to Foreigners. In that year, he met David Jakoby Hirsch, a German Jew who had converted to Christianity. There was a quality in Hirsch that Baylee admired, so he invited him to begin a missionary for the Germans in Liverpool. To begin with, the German Church that was rented on Rathbone Street was a branch of the Anglican Church. Hirsch ran it with two elders.

The national trait for organisation united many families into a community with its own schools. The German-speaking one on Scotland Road began with 45 children and quickly expanded to 100. Another school in Bold Street, which opened in 1865, did well enough to attract the sons and daughters of gentlefolk from the wider community. It didn't close until the outbreak of World War I.

Pork butchers from the Hohenlohe area (north east of Stuttgart) strung together the sausages of home. The fruity smell of baking pastry and the steam from sauerkraut joined the air of a city already rich in aromas. Immigrants tend to do what they would have done in the own countries. Some of the beer houses on Scotland Road belonged to German families. Many of their compatriots worked in the sugar factories.

By 1850, there was a self-sufficient German church with a congregation of merchants and factory workers who used a chapel, bought for £850, in Sir Thomas Street. Twenty-two years later, the congregation bought Newington Chapel in Renshaw Street for £3,330. This became the German Church in Liverpool.

As the Germans grew in numbers, their hard work, high educational standards and friendly manners won the respect of local people. However, there were tensions between the immigrants themselves, often caused by doctrinal differences.

By 1880, part of north Liverpool was called 'Little Germany', but all was to change in 1914 with the outbreak of war. By that time, the German Church had a congregation of 1000 of whom 549, mostly children, had been born in the country. There were 67 pork butchers, 16 sugar factory workers, 13 in trade and business and 7 publicans. There were also many other Germans on Merseyside who were not attached to the church.

A hostile mood swept through the city. The school in Bold Street and a seaman's hostel closed. Many people lost their jobs. After the sinking of the *Lusitania* with the loss of 1,200 lives on 7 May 1915, anti-German riots broke out. Some 250 women and children were sent back to Germany. The church held monthly meetings, but the name 'German Church, Liverpool' was erased and the rooms were rented out to international Bible students. Even so, the congregation was resilient and activities resumed after the war. In 1930, they sold their building in Renshaw Street for £14,000 and bought a church in Canning Street for £4000.

Hitler's rise led to renewed hostility against the German community in Liverpool, and some Germans returned home in anticipation of trouble. Others were sent to internment camps on the Isle of Man at the outbreak of war. While they were away, their church was almost destroyed by the bombing raids on Liverpool docks.

After World War II, there was a determination to revive the community again. From 1951, the smaller congregation met at the back of the Princes Gate Baptist Church, Toxteth. Then the new £6000 church was built on the site of the old one. It was dedicated on 13 December 1959. All their services are conducted in German, but there is a great affection for this country, despite what Hermine diplomatically refers to as their "understandable" treatment during the wars. "We love England," she said. "It doesn't mean that we don't love Germany, but there is a different feeling of togetherness here, in our church." There is a certain amount of ribbing about football and the war. "But immigrants must be thick-skinned. You just have to laugh at it," she said.

The conversation switches to the 1960s when the Beatles visited clubs in Hamburg, beginning a cultural exchange which continues today, with Germans prominent among Liverpool's tourists. "This city has something to offer although it is messy," said Hermine. "After a year or two, you love Liverpool. There is a spirit here. The people are not as fussy. In Germany, everything has to be done just like that."

Pastor Gunter estimates that some 22,000 people born in Germany now live in the North West, including the Liverpool footballers Dietmar Hamann, Markus Babbel and Christian Ziege.

In the Liverpool Church, a Christmas tree from North Wales is placed to the right of the Cross. The simple decorations remind them of the warmth of home. "It is the same when we sing *Stille Nacht*," said Pastor Gunter.

And their silent prayers, heard only by God, are said in German.

KEY DATES

1821: Services and prayer meetings held for German seamen in Liverpool.

1846: Liverpool German Church in Rathbone Street founded as a branch of the Anglican Church.

1872: The Congregation buys Newington Chapel, Renshaw Street, as its new church.

1876: Links are severed with Anglican Church.

1904: German congregations in the UK form an association.

1906: Sugar slump forces many Germans to leave Liverpool, but the number of butchers increases.

1930: Congregations buys church in Canning Street to replace Renshaw Street building.

1940: Canning Street Church damaged during Blitz.

1959: New Canning Street church opens.

1970: Concern that German migration to Liverpool has almost stopped, though the community is determined to carry on.

1977: Liverpool and Manchester become a single pastorate.

1996: 150th anniversary of the German Church in Liverpool.

THE GREEK COMMUNITY

At a barber's shop in Prescot Street where he has cut the hair of filmstars and footballers over the years, David Moustaka speaks of the splendours of the Greek community and their church.

~

When he steadies the heads of the famous, the barber with the perfectly trimmed moustache sometimes feels like a priest listening to the secrets of those who stare into the mirrors on the walls of his shop. Of course, the barber holds an advantage over the priest because he can see the faces of the men who open their hearts to him, but both honour the rule of confidentiality. The hair is swept from the floor, the stray stubble brushed from the confessant's collar, and the case is closed, without recourse to penance.

David Moustaka is one of the most respected businessmen on Merseyside. The traditional symbol of blood and teeth outside his shop tells the customers that he is a real gentleman's barber and not one of those "unisex hairdressers" who create styles, rather than simply pruning uneven hairs. To win the respect of the citizens in a new country should be important to all immigrants and it is a code that has served David well.

He was the fifth of six children born to Michael and Maria Moustaka in the village of Paralimni, Cyprus. His father was a foreman on the docks. During

David's childhood, Cyprus was a British Crown colony. Life was hard on the island. Many young people sought a life elsewhere. At the age of 16, David decided to join his married sister, Paraskevi, in Southgate, London, where he began his apprenticeship as a hairdresser in Marble Arch. In 1964, he married Irene Nambrianides and the couple decided to move to Liverpool where Paraskevi had moved with another sister, Christina.

The city was going crazy. It was at the zenith of its post-war popularity, with Everton and Liverpool riding high to the rhythms of the Beatles, the Searchers and the other Merseybeat groups. These were extraordinary times for a barber.

"When I first came to England, the styles were like they are today," said David. "They were short and tidy and people used to get their hair cut regularly. They wanted their necks to be clean. Then the long hair came in. But long hair needs a lot of care, so we still got a lot of custom. All the styles leave their mark, so you still have people who cling to the older styles – crew cuts and the longer hair."

The footballers were among David's regular customers: Kevin Keegan, Kenny Dalglish, Phil Neal, Ray Clemence, Brian Labone, Gordon West. The mainstay of his business has always been the business and professional class, with occasional visits from showbiz stars performing in the city. "A barber's shop is a meeting-place," David said. "You have a customer in the chair for half an hour and you have a conversation. They tell you their problems and you listen. It is similar to being a priest."

Like many Greeks, 62-year-old David believes that material success has to be tempered with spiritual strength if a man is to feel good within himself.

His countrymen have been coming to Merseyside since 1810. The early settlers merged into the general population, but as the century progressed and their numbers increased, the Greeks, led by cotton traders and merchants, became more community conscious. In common with the Chinese, the Jews, the Scandinavians and the black population, they gathered on the docks, spreading up to what is now Liverpool 8.

Meanwhile, Manchester's Greeks were building their own church, The Annunciation, which was consecrated in 1861. At that time, the Liverpool Greeks worshipped in a spacious ground-floor room, which they rented in Sefton Park. They had to travel to Manchester for the great feasts. The president of the Greek Community in Liverpool was George Michael Papayiannis, who, in 1855, founded the Elerman and Papayiannis Navigational Company, which soon had seven steam-ships.

Then, as now, Manchester's triumphs were resented in Liverpool. The audacious shipping magnate called a meeting in October 1863, which resulted in money being raised for the building of the Greek Orthodox Church in Princes Road. The Liverpool-based architect, Mr G Potessaro, charged no fee for his design of a magnificent four-domed structure in the Byzantine fashion. The builder Henry Summers won the commission and the church was finished in 1870 and named St Nicholas to honour the patron saint of sailors. The building was consecrated on 4 January 1871, with full Eastern rites by His Grace Alexandros Lycourgos, Archbishop of Syra and Tinos, who had travelled from Constantinople as part of his mission to try to unite all the Christian churches. The Archbishops of York and Canterbury were present. Although Liverpool would not be a city for another ten years, its importance to the British Empire was recognised far afield.

About 300 Greeks had settled on Merseyside and it seemed that their population would prosper and grow. However, this was an age of adventure and the temptations of distant lands were hard to resist. By the beginning of the twentieth century, many Greeks were emigrating to Australia, America, Europe and Egypt. It was a lean time. In 1933, the Most Reverend Archimandrides Nichofforos Yiannoulis returned to Greece because his congregation had almost disappeared. A priest from Manchester conducted one service a month at the church built on the faith of God-fearing people in a strange land.

After World War II, the community began to recover, as British soldiers brought home Greek brides. Some Armenian Serbs and Romanians helped swell the congregation. People from other denominations began to admire the Orthodox celebrations, particularly the Great Feast of Easter when local children would be given red eggs and other gifts. The recovery was in full flush by the mid-1960s. Cypriots had left their homes during the independence struggle. There was a priest again at St Nicholas's, and a young barber had just moved into his shop in Prescot Street.

"There are about one thousand eight hundred Greeks here, the majority of whom are Cypriots," said David Moustaka. "Liverpool has been a good home to Greek people. The majority of us have done well. I think we are well liked, too. I have made a lot of friends. I play golf at Lee Park (Netherley) and have met a lot of people there."

David and Irene had two children who are now in their thirties. Son, Michael, renovates and rents property and daughter, Helen, is a travel consultant. For the past three years, David has been the church's president. One of his jobs is to light a slow-burning candle in a glass in front of the altar. This is a place of wonder. The sun is high and its light comes through the 12 stained-glass windows of the dome, circling up from a ceiling painted in the blue of Our Lady.

David shakes his head. How on Earth did they transport the eight pillars of Penteli marble from Greece to here? Some miracles are of man's own making. The original icons, too, came from Greece. Jesus is in the middle, St Nicholas is to the left of the mother and child, and John the Baptist is to the right. Glass stretches across the feet of these icons where the women once kissed them, leaving lipstick stains, which were hard to remove. Small paintings of the figures are now fixed under the main icons. These can be sponged clean. All the services here are conducted in Greek.

"It's as it was two thousand years ago," said David. "We haven't changed anything. The service takes over three hours. Obviously, before you take Holy Communion, you have to prepare yourself to receive the body of Jesus. For three or four days you cannot eat certain things and, of course, you have to confess before taking Holy Communion.

"We get an average of one hundred and fifty people coming here for services from all over the region, but a lot more come for the festivals, like Easter and Christmas and the saints' days."

There is a throne to the right side of the red-carpeted aisle. "You have to be at least a bishop to sit there," says David, as he pads down the thick-pile of the red carpet.

Greek business helped build the church. Now their successors support it. Michael Sergi was president before David. He was a big name in catering and property on Merseyside. His son Jimmy has taken over the business now and he is the church's treasurer.

At the back of the building is a bowl filled with Crosses, fashioned from pine leaves. These were used during the Palm Sunday service.

There is a knock on the door. Two little girls, one Christian and blonde, the other Muslim and dark, want to take a peep inside. David opens the door. "It's amazing," says the blonde. David nods in agreement.

"This is a very fine country. I've always been happy here."

KEY DATES

1810: Greek traders begin visiting Liverpool, but they don't form a settled community.

1846: Prosperous merchants and traders start a Greek community.

1861: Liverpool Greeks admit to being jealous of The Annunciation Church built by Manchester's Greeks.

1863: Prominent Greeks, led by the shipping owner George Michael Papayiannis, decide to build their own church in Liverpool.

1870: The church, only the second custom-built Orthodox Greek Church in the UK, is finished.

1871: The church is consecrated by the Archbishop of Syra and Tinos.

Early 1900s: Greek population drops.

1933: The priest at St Nicholas's returns to Greece as the congregation almost disappears.

1945: Gradual increase in the population as World War II soldiers bring home Greek brides.

1957: Greek businessmen pay for extensive repairs to their church.

1960: Cyprus granted independence from Britain after years of unrest.

1970 onwards: Greek population on Merseyside continues to rise.

THE ITALIAN COMMUNITY

At the Italian Consulate, Birkenhead, some Italians meet for coffee and biscuits and remember when they first arrived in this country, bringing with them their glorious food, romance and love of opera.

~

When the wind comes up from the river, confetti from town hall weddings swirl down the street gathering in the doorway of the Italian Consulate, which lies beneath the fluttering green, white and red flag. It is appropriate that it should be so. This stout, stone building celebrates the coming of the world's most romantic travellers to the banks of the Mersey. Inside, the men are drinking dark coffee, eating digestive biscuits and talking about women – a good subject for people always touched by the passions of the heart.

These days, Italian girls are slim and willowy as they sweep down the streets in their elegant dresses and subtle scents, says Angelo Vicarello, with an appreciative smile. Once, they were short and tubby because they ate too much pasta and didn't take enough exercise. "Hmm, that was the idea of Benito Mussolini. He thought that Italian women should have wide hips for child-bearing," replied Nunzia Bertali, consul to the Italian people on Merseyside.

Mussolini, puffed with ambition for a second Roman Empire, was to blame for many of his country's ills. On a happier note, though, his unwise entry into World War II was indirectly responsible for these people being in Mrs Bertali's office and now discussing the contribution made by Italians to the well-being of the region.

They came here in the 1950s when their country was in deep, economic depression following the ravages of the war. A deal had been arranged between the Italian Government and our National Coal Board, which needed men aged between 18 and 31. About 3000 Italians accepted the offer and settled in communities around the old pits on the Lancashire coalfield, including Sutton Manor, Astley Green, and Bold. So, from the sunshine and swollen water-melons of southern Italy and Sicily, they found themselves with torches on their helmets, hacking out coal, or running the trolleys in those depths where there has never been a dawn. Others broke the frozen ground with their shovels and pick-axes on farms. Whether they were over ground or under, it was hard work for tough men.

These were not the matinee idol-style Italians, the Valentinos of the long mirrors in their wide suits with the slicked-backed hair, but men who were hungry and worried, in a country that had been first devastated and then drained by war. Families were close and if they could support their loved ones, even by going overseas, it had to be done.

Now they are a happy and prosperous group, sitting in the office of their consulate, just off Hamilton Square, Birkenhead. There is poetry in their very names: Angelo Vacarello, Giuseppe Tummino, Maria Persichelli Castrianni, Francesco Bracchitta, Concetta Bracchitta, Vincenzo Baio, Serafina Graceffa Parello, Angelo Candiano, Giuseppe Candiano, Giuseppe Sereni, Salavtore Di Stefano and Enza Baio.

"I was eighteen and I had never been away from home before, said Mr Vacarello, whose Sicilian father had worked in sulphur mines and farms. "But Italy then wasn't like it is now. It was very hard. There weren't many jobs. All the lads wanted to go abroad."

When they arrived in England, the Italians lived in a hostel.

"We went to the pub and the dance hall," he recalled. "Nobody bothered us. The weather in England then wasn't like it is today. It was foggy. If you stood by a wall in Liverpool, it was black. It has changed. Living in England now is like living in heaven." Angelo, who married an English girl called Maureen Guest, worked in the mines for 17 years before moving near to the Vauxhall car factory in Ellesmere Port, where he worked on the production lines.

A smiling Salvatore Di Stefano walks across the room. This 73-year-old Sicilian still has the shoulders of a middle-weight boxing champion. After spells in Nottinghamshire and Yorkshire, he came to Liverpool in 1955. "After the coal mines, when I was sixty-six, I opened a greengrocery on the East Lancs Road," he said. Salvatore is now retired.

"I found it a bit cold when I first came here. But I have enjoyed every minute. I was single for three years – it was really marvellous; working, dancing, all over the place."

The Italian economy improved rapidly during the 1950s, leading to the 'miracle' of the 1960s, based on cars, Vespa and Lambretta scooters, engineering and electrical goods and, of course, Sophia Loren and Gina Lollobrigida. All those in Mrs Bertali's office said they were pleased to have settled in the UK. Although the miners made their mark, Italians have been coming to Liverpool since the eighteenth century. The early arrivals tended to come from the professions, music, the arts, engineering, skilled trades and business. These people left the various states, which were not unified into a nation until 1861.

Italians are popularly associated with ice cream, restaurants and snack bars. Mrs Bertali thinks this is because their shops occupy prominent positions on the high street. The others melted into the general community and were quickly assimilated.

Milan-born Mrs Bertali came to Merseyside in 1982 with her husband Alberto, now vice-chairman of the Hoover group. She is doing some research on the early Italians. For example, the Casartelli factory, precision engineers who specialised in meteorological instruments, had factories in Liverpool and Manchester. However, it was different after World War II.

"You have to bear in mind that, in Italy at that time, there was no money and no food," she said. "You had to go wherever you could if you wanted to survive and do something with your life. So the young people were given the opportunity to work abroad and earn some money. This is very important. These people were starving. Their motivation was survival." Hunger feeds ambition. The women supported their husbands with loyalty and determination, patience and kindness, fervently believing that they were building a strong base for their children.

"The majority of these people had to prove to their families at home that they had been successful here," she said. "They sent money home and they continued to do so. In this way, they made a great contribution to Italy as well. We now have about four thousand Italians on Merseyside."

Now they are talking about Italian women again. "They were pear-shaped," the consul agreed. "That was because of Fascism. Mussolini wanted the women to bear children. In order to do so, they weren't allowed to do any sports and they ate pasta. He wanted to increase the population, so that Italy would become a big country."

Giuseppe Sereni, still handsome at 72, is from Tuscany. He and Luisa have two sons, Antonio, the Birkenhead-based defence solicitor, and Giancarlo, who is also a solicitor. In the true Italian style, they all speak with pride and affection about their children.

He didn't like the English food when he arrived. He gestures disapprovingly, stretching the arms of his smart brown corduroy suit. "It was terrible," he said. "There was so many cakes and sweets. We were used to spaghetti and macaroni, fruit and vegetables." Some of the Italians were so unhappy about the diet that they persuaded the local doctors to issue prescriptions for olive oil, which was supplied in the chemists' shops.

"But it was July and the weather was lovely and we went in the park," he added. "Of course, we had to learn the English language and we went to a school. A priest came to the school. After a few months, things weren't bad at all. It was a lovely country. We met some nice people. Everyone welcomed us. We found some good girlfriends as well, especially in St Helens."

They're all talking together, remembering the old times. The families are scattered now and they don't meet as often, so this is a happy occasion for them. He smiles as the women laugh across the table. "Well, you gotta tell the truth!" he smiles.

KEY DATES

Late eighteenth century: Italian masons and other skilled tradesmen come to work in Liverpool.

1851: Census of Liverpool shows the influence of Italians on the port. There are musicians, opticians, gilders, carvers, French polishers, mariners, a doctor, language professors and an advocate.

1861: Italy unified under Emmanuel II.

1915: Italy joined World War I on the Allied side, suffering appalling losses.

1918: Despite being on the victorious side, Italy feels that it gets a raw deal in the peace settlement. Thousands leave their country seeking prosperity in the New World. Some stay in the UK, opening restaurants and ice cream parlours.

1919: Gabriele D'Annunzio seizes Trieste from the Austrians.

1922: Benito Mussolini assumes power and establishes a Fascist state.

1936: Italy conquers Ethiopia and Albania.

1940: Italy enters World War II on the German side, but in a disastrous series of military reverses loses its African empire.

1943: Mussolini deposed. Italy surrenders and joins the Allies, but the country is invaded by the Germans.

1944: Rome falls to the Allies.

1951: Thousands of Italians seek work in the UK, many becoming miners or farm labourers in the North West.

1985: Thirty-nine Juventus fans killed in disturbance at the Heysel Stadium, Brussels, before the European Cup Final against Liverpool.

A TIME TO MOURN

DAILY POST

North West Merseyside

Wednesday, September 11, 2002   Weather: Mainly dry   www.icliverpool.co.uk   32p

**DATELINE: DAWN
SEPTEMBER 11 2001**

REMEMBER

Once you built the towers
made them high,
Your tiers of hope piercing
the sky,
Your girders of might over
Liberty's shore

Now they are gone
lost to our sight,
Yet, in memory's true hold still
may they rise,
Shining on, called by our faith
in the skies.

**DATELINE: DAWN
SEPTEMBER 11 2002**

Most of the of these articles need little introduction. A loss is the same, whether publicly known or privately mourned, but I have found that Merseyside unites in times of both joy and of sadness.

9/11

The then editor of the *Daily Post*, Alastair Machray, wanted to do something special to commemorate the first anniversary of September the 11th. Some of us gathered in his office to discuss ideas. I suggested a piece linking Liverpool to New York. He liked the idea, but thought we needed a special front page with a poem.

A number of established poets were asked to submit poems on the subject. We didn't like any of them. So, by September 9th when things should have been well advanced, almost nothing had been achieved. Rather foolishly, I said I would have a go at writing a poem myself that night. Meanwhile, Stephen Shakeshaft, the picture editor, and Tony Ellis, the assistant editor, began designing the front page. The next morning we all met again. I read some lines, which I had scribbled on the back of a cigarette packet. To my surprise, everyone liked the lines and it was decided to run them as a poem on the front page with photographs of the New York Skyline.

Remember
Once you built the towers
Made them high,
Your tiers of hope piercing
The sky,
Your girders of might over
Liberty's shore

Now they are gone
Lost to our sight,
Yet, in memory's true hold, still
May they rise,
Shining on, called by our faith
In the skies.

ATLANTIC OVERTURE

The dream came first, scattering its seeds across the cobbled quays of the growing port, and the seeds were the people from many lands, separated by their gods, their costumes and their languages. But they were bonded as one in their desire to cast off the old ways and to reach together in faith for a new beginning, free from fear and hunger and persecution. Yes, it was a dream, the biggest the world had ever known. It has given the great Atlantic cities of Liverpool and New York a common heritage, which has matured into a culture of history, humour and song that can never be broken.

Both were havens for the dispossessed. Both gave those disparate people a place in the world and a sense of belonging. The people from the two ports, who had seen so much, became tough, proud, quick-tongued, at once cynical and sentimental. It set them apart from the mainstream of their countries, made them entertaining, a little arrogant maybe, defiant, wary of authority, and always conscious of what went before: those memories left in the lands of their ancestors.

To be a New Yorker, or a to be a Liverpudlian, is to be different. Perhaps their citizens have more in common with each other than they do with their fellow countrymen. So today, when the world remembers those who died in the attacks on the World Trade Center, emotions distilled in an ancestral understanding, as well as natural affection and sympathy, will cross 3,500 miles of turbulent ocean from Liverpool to New York.

Since that deed of evil, which left some 2,800 bodies in the rubble of the world's tallest building which reached almost a quarter mile into the sky, the links have been even stronger. Our firefighters have joined their brothers in New York at the site of Ground Zero, linking arms over the place where it happened and where nothing is left, except the spirit of the people.

The mood of our tourists – going to see the Statue of Liberty, the Empire State Buildings, Carnegie Hall and the Lincoln Center – is a little more sombre these days, respecting the feelings of a people who have demonstrated an almost British resilience in the face of adversity.

When they come here, contemplating their past – to see the cathedrals, the haunts of the Beatles and the grand old buildings – they know they are being greeted by friends. These are the people whose ancestors knew the smell of the fruit in crates on the waterfront, whose hands were burned by the same lines of rope secured to the stages at either end of the great voyage.

Now these ties established in friendship are to be made official. Mike Storey, leader of Liverpool City Council, said yesterday that arrangements are being made for the cities to be formally twinned. All eight million New Yorkers are also to be given the freedom of Liverpool.

In the telephone directory, the names of people from distant lands are listed in alphabetical order – Isaacs, Jones, Karpinski, McNair, Mohamed, Offerman, O'Reilly, Rodriguez, Rossi, Wineberg, Woo. Their forebears came to Liverpool and New York with hope as an ideal. Many settled in our city, moving from the cellars and lodging houses on the Mersey waterfront. Others awaited a Yankee clipper, or in later years, a steam-ship, to carry them to the promised land. It is estimated that in the 100 years from 1840 more than nine million people left Liverpool for New York, making homes in the five boroughs of Manhattan, the Bronx, Brooklyn, Queens and Staten Island.

Manhattan Island had been bought in 1626 from the native Indians by the Dutch West India Company who founded New Amsterdam. Thirty-eight years later, the British took the colony, renaming it New York. So began the modern history of a city, inextricably linked to Liverpool.

It took about six weeks for a sailing craft to cross the ocean, if the weather permitted. The advent of steam changed that. Cunard's first ship, the paddle steamer *Britannia*, made her maiden voyage on 4 July, Independence Day, 1840. With a service speed of nine knots, she carried 115 passengers to Halifax, Nova Scotia, in 12 days. She took another 46 hours to reach Boston. By the end of the decade, Cunard was making regular trips to New York.

Many were fleeing disasters and persecution – the Irish potato famine of the 1840s, the pogroms which beset Russia and Poland in the 1880s, crop failures and war.

To mark the USA's centenary in 1876, France gave them the Statue of Liberty. To the Jewish poet, Emma Lazarus, this great copper woman with the torch, standing at 300ft over New York harbour, was the Mother of Exiles. In 1883, she wrote The New Colossus, which was inscribed on the statue:

Give me your tired, your poor,
Your huddled masses, yearning to breathe free,
The wretched refuse of your teeming shore,
Send those, the homeless, the tempest-tossed to me:
I lift my lamp beside the golden door.

Ellis Island acted as the main US immigration centre from 1892 to 1943, at its height processing one million people annually. During the last century, sailors returned to Liverpool with stories of New York's irrepressible drive, its invention, its charm, its crazy, cosmopolitan nature. This was the city of Scott Fitzgerald and his Jazz Age flappers, Lorenz Hart, George and Ira Gershwin, and Damon Runyon, whose characters brought glamour and humour to the underworld.

Among those growing up in this atmosphere were Ida and Israel Bernstein, who had left Lukshivka, a 'shtetl', or village, near Kiev. They adopted Sid Bernstein. Now he is the revered impresario and writer from East 72nd Street and one of Liverpool's cultural ambassadors. As the man who introduced the Beatles to New York in 1964, the 84-year-old crosses the ocean regularly, loving both cities in equal measure. To him, both are home.

Sid had been brought up with the sounds from the big shows and then the Brill Building in Broadway, home of Tin Pan Alley. There, in tiny cubicles, Carole King, Neil Sedaka, Leiber and Stoller, Doc Pomus and others, composed the songs sung by a generation. But New York's golden age of pop, epitomised by the extraordinary harmonies of the Four Seasons, quailed before the British 'invasion' led by the Beatles. In February 1964, thousands of girls greeted them at the John F Kennedy International Airport.

Then, the cities were joined in celebration of a common culture. Today, they are united in sorrow. The people of Liverpool, who suffered terrible losses in the bombing of war, reach out to the New Yorkers, who suffered their grievous loss in a time of peace.

Mike Storey said: "There is a blood link, a link of life between the two cities. And September the eleventh has brought us closer. The thoughts of our people go to those of New York."

Chris Leahey, an accountant, his wife Margaret and their three young children, are friends of the Storeys. They moved to New York from Liverpool two years ago. Their new city was selected by the terrorists as a symbol of Western capitalism and greed, but to the Leaheys it has become a warm and friendly home, quite different from its popular image on TV.

In the history of all things, there is joy and there is tragedy. On 8 December 1980, John Lennon was shot dead by Mark Chapman outside the Dakota Building, where he lived with Yoko and their son Sean. To his memory, the Strawberry Fields garden was opened in Central Park, New York. Visitors from both cities, and the rest of the world, lay flowers by the oak tree planted there. Sid Bernstein (always pronounced 'Bernsteen' in Liverpool and New York) has happier memories of the former Beatle.

"You see, he lived on West Seventy-Second Street, where the Dakota is, and I live on East Seventy-Second Street, just across the park," said Sid. "So we would meet once in a while, just by accident, on Columbus Avenue. We would always say a very warm hello. In fact, there was one occasion when he introduced me to Yoko. She said, 'John, how many times are you going to introduce me to Sid?'. Sometimes we would meet when he was with his little boy. He liked New York, John Lennon. But I like Liverpool. There is a spirit and love there which I am very attached to."

To some, the defiance of the New Yorkers has been an inspiring example. David Balmer and John Cash, both Wallasey firefighters, policemen Andrew Davies and Alan Landrun, security guard Graham Farrell and the former New York firefighter Ron Schancke, were treated like heroes when they went to the USA to raise money for relatives of the 343 brothers in the New York Fire Department who lost their lives. They walked the 286 miles from the Pentagon in Washington DC to Ground Zero, making £26,000 for the fund. Ron, who left the USA nine years ago, is now a Merseyside ambulance technician.

A cross, fashioned from the final girder removed from Ground Zero, is being collected by Frank Proctor, the 52-year-old boss of the Many Happy Returns Travel agency in Ainsdale. The 12-inch stretch of iron belonged to Stephen Vendola, an employee of the New York Port Authority, which owned the World Trade Center. He rented a holiday villa in Orlando, Florida, owned by Frank's brother Kevin.

Kevin, a BT manager in Liverpool, said, "I would have conversations with Stephen and his family after September the eleventh, telling them that the people over here were thinking about the people of New York." As a result, Stephen had the cross delivered to the villa, where it is being collected by Frank. "The final girder was like an icon in America, symbolising September the eleventh," said Kevin. "Stephen and some of his colleagues were given parts of the girder. He had his welded into the cross. The brothers' cousin, Father Gerry Proctor, of Saint Margaret Mary's Church, is going to bless it."

Today, our cities, for centuries washed by the same waters, will be as one in a spirit of remembrance.

HILLSBOROUGH THIRTEEN YEARS ON

April 15th, 2002. The names of the dead were read out one by one and when they ran off the first page of the programme, the sound of turning paper rose from the Kop like a great flapping of birds' wings. This was Anfield, the famous football ground turned briefly into a church, dedicated to the memory of the 96 Liverpool supporters who died at Hillsborough.

No other British city remembers its dead like Liverpool. There's a tradition of passion and affection expressed with a defiant emotion, which says quite simply: "If you belonged to us once, you belong to us always."

Yesterday, more than 2,000 people filed into the ground for the service to mark the 13th anniversary of the disaster. Among them was Gerard Houllier, the club's manager, who walked through a turnstile to the main stand, leading players past and present to their places among the ordinary supporters in the Kop. Their dark suits and club ties contrasted with the vivid red of the flip-back plastic seats overlooking the pitch being prepared for tomorrow's match between England and Paraguay.

Although this was a time of mourning, the fans came in their colours – most in the red of Liverpool, but some in the blue of Everton. For, in their remembrance of Hillsborough, the two proud clubs have been as one. They sat in clusters, or in couples, up the steep rise of the stand. Below them, with their backs to the goal were the 42 boys from the St Francis Xavier College, Woolton, in their mauve gowns and white surplices. With voices ranging from treble to bass, they opened the service at 2.30pm by singing Samuel Barber's *Adagio*. People were still coming quietly in, and below them, to the left of the choir, they could see the 96 candles which would be lit singly as the names were spoken.

Almost everyone on Merseyside was touched by Hillsborough. Ninety-six deaths and hundreds of injuries have made thousands of stories of luck and sorrow and bravery.

Keith Knowles, a season ticket holder at Anfield, still wonders if one of the candles should have been for him. As head of music at the college, he was conducting the boys down there by the turf. He is also a fervent Liverpudlian. He had intended to go to the semi-final between Liverpool and Nottingham Forest, but his grandfather thought it would be wiser to save his money for the Cup Final at Wembley. They had been going to matches together for 22 years. "Because of that, this occasion means a lot to me emotionally and personally," said Keith. "Friends of mine were there, people I went to school with. So, I have been able to tell the boys in the choir a lot about what it means to us all."

Keith's grandfather, Ray Ellison, who died in 1998, was a Liverpool fan for 72 years. He was also a fully qualified football referee and a school teacher in the city.

"The music we picked for today got across the meaning of the event with great dignity," Keith said. "It is a privilege doing this for the city of Liverpool." Keith guided the boys into *Abide with Me* and everyone stood up. Then three local clergymen, Rev Derek Bibb, Rev Kelvin Bolton and Father Desmond Power, began reading the names.

They came in alphabetical, in batches of 20, after which the boys sang, *May the Choir of Angels Be Ever with You* – May you rest in paradise. They did that four times, until there were just 16 names left. The last one, Graham John Wright, was said seconds before the minute's silence began at 3.06pm. That was when the match at Hillsborough was abandoned with the dead and dying crushed against the railings at the Leppings Lane terrace.

Trevor Hicks, chairman of the Hillsborough Family Support Group, who lost two daughters in the disaster, spoke after the silence, calling on the authorities to reject any suggestion that fans should be allowed to stand on the terraces again. People listened quietly, appreciating his references to their 13-year struggle for justice against those responsible for the deaths.

Then the crowd stood, with scarves and banners high, to sing *You'll Never Walk Alone,* a song which could have been written for such an occasion.

Mr Houllier stood in his camel coat with a cream scarf wrapped around his neck against the cold which persisted despite the unbroken sunshine. All around him, people began to clap, praising his courage in returning to work after heart bypass surgery. He was followed by the highly-paid stars – Emile Heskey, Gary McAllister, Patrik Berger, Nick Barmby, Marcus Babbel and Vladimire Smicer, and the favourite from an earlier team, Ian Rush.

Outside, on the railings by the eternal flame at the Bill Shankly gates, were the flowers left by Brian Thompson to his friends who died on that April afternoon, Marion McCabe – who was 21, and Inger Shah, 38.

"I come here every year," he said. "Inger and Marion were very good friends. We stood on the Kop together. Hillsborough will never be forgotten in this city."

IN MEMORY OF JAMES – TEN YEARS ON

He was just a little boy with blue eyes. None of us knew him then, but soon his name would be familiar to people right across the country and even further than that. James Bulger and the terrible things that had been done to him were about to touch all parents.

Now, when you take your child to the places where children once played unsupervised, their innocent songs and yells filling the air, free from the constraints of adults, you hear only a strange silence. How could we have understood then that the murder of James would bring fear to mothers and fathers, without regard to class or background.

The impossible had happened, an event too terrible to contemplate. A boy had been killed by two other children. So, when we walk with our sons and daughters in the shopping centre, the park, the beach, we look more carefully, perhaps sensing danger, though there is really nothing to fear, and we squeeze their hands a little tighter, lest they should run off. In that sense, James Bulger will always be with us, a face on a poster, carrying a chilling reminder.

Of course, we hadn't learned to think like that on the night of 12 February 1993. I was the night news editor on the *Daily Post*, drinking coffee from plastic beakers with my colleague and friend, Richard Elias, the duty reporter. It had been an uneventful shift and we were looking forward to starting the weekend. But I asked Richard to check on the missing toddler when he was making his routine calls to the emergency services.

Surprisingly enough at the time, missing children were not very unusual. My opinion was that we should record it, advising people what they should do if they had any information that could help the police. But when he came off the phone, Richard was clearly worried. He had been told something by one of the contacts that he had made with the police. Richard's already keen instincts had been stirred. To begin with, the missing boy was only two. Now, the main search for him had moved from the area of the New Strand shopping centre, Bootle, where he had gone missing, to the towpath of the Liverpool/Leeds Canal. Dozens of officers were involved and they were talking about calling in an underwater search unit.

"I have a gut feeling about this," said Richard. "It's more than a missing child. I fear the worst."

I trusted Richard's instincts and spoke to the then night editor, John Williams, who almost immediately agreed that it should be our 'splash' – the newspaper word for the front-page lead. Thus, under the headline 'Fears Grow For Toddler', we carried the story, using a photograph of James, a face that in the coming days would be seen by millions.

It is sometimes said that journalism is a hard, rather soulless profession, in which the individual ambitions of those chasing a story over-ride the feelings of others. That might have been true of some of those assigned the Bulger story, but the journalists I knew were deeply moved. In the office, and later in the pubs, we spoke often of what had happened and asked why? At such times it is hard not to be subjective. Then a haunting question comes and lingers. What if it had happened to ...? In more philosophical moments we even contemplated the nature of life: "Are some people born bad?" "Was it as simple as that?" we asked. "Were the two young boys who killed James irredeemably wicked?" None of us had the temerity to offer an answer. Such judgements are for higher places.

At the time of James's murder, I was newly married, hoping that one day I would have a son of my own. Exactly three years later, I became a father – maybe a little too possessive, ever proud.

But what of little James, the blue-eyed boy, led by the hand to his death by those two older boys? Well, he will always be with us, his head cocked to one side and smiling, ever warning parents to be vigilant.

When I take my son to the shops and my wife says, "Don't let him out of your sight", it is in memory of James. We all do it. Instead of letting our sons or daughters play on their own with the other children in the park, we stand and watch. That is what James Bulger means to us all. We will never forget what happened to him. As Richard Elias said all those years ago: "It's more than a missing child. I fear the worst."

MY MOTHER

Even when they squeezed the needle into her arm, now purple with bruises and very thin, trying to find a vein to carry the morphine's peace into her being like the slow creep of night, she said, "Thank you, my dear" and she smiled in her old way, full of the graciousness of her years.

And then the sleep came and she went again to some place that you can only imagine. Maybe, she was back in the shelter outside Lloyd's Bank. Here, the blue number two bus carried her into town to the department store with the café that was reached by a brown, creaking lift and attended by a man dull of wit but quick to smile, who pushed the button to the second floor. There, on the green leather chairs studded in brass, all the ladies gathered over coffee and cigarettes, leaving their lipstick on the cork-tips. Stubbing the ends into a small hill in dimpled-glass trays and gossiping all the while, their sharp eyes squinted behind the smoke and steam that curled into a warm fug by the ceiling's lazy fans.

Suddenly, my mother would wake again in the hospital, where the curtains were closed around her bed. One of us would plump-up the pillows to make her more comfortable. "She is listening to everything you say," said a nurse. Hearing is the last thing to go." So we talked together, about all the banal things that make up life, like my struggle to catch the pet rabbit on the lawn. 'Granny' had given my son the rabbit for his seventh birthday two weeks before. "One of these days, I would like to watch them play in the garden," she had said. Now, she wouldn't see them together; not in the keen light of our days, anyway.

They had said to me on the telephone that she was going. Would we like to be there, beside her in these closing hours? My wife and I were joined by my mother's eldest daughter and her eldest granddaughter at the bedside. Together, we spoke of the old times, when she would be in the kitchen, amid the smell of baking bread or cakes, in a pinny, wiping the perspiration from her brow with the back of her hand; a rolling-pin on the red table-top, threatening to squash the resistance from a recalcitrant lump of pastry, as the awaiting coke glowed behind the chapel-brown of the ancient Aga.

My mother, lying there on the bed, was 94. Below the ward window I noticed they had strung a net between the walls to keep out the pigeons. Feathers hung on the webbing. "Would you like a drink of tea?" we asked. She nodded and my wife held her head, brushing away the grey hair, to pour the tea from a plastic beaker.

"That's nice."

Tea was always important to my mother. Moments of celebration and grief were confirmed in the family memory by 'a nice cup of tea' – not then the miserable powder held in perforated bags, but real, loose tea, as dark as a mahogany cabinet. I am sure that, on her arrival in North Wales, where she had been evacuated during the war with her three daughters, she would have put on the kettle. You introduced yourself to a new home with the hiss of steam.

"You know," she said, with mock coyness a few weeks ago. "I think the butcher in the village must have taken a bit of a notion to me. He always added something extra to our rations."

So, the war was fought on the home-front, but far away her husband was in a prison camp. For a long time, he was missing, presumed dead. My mother became a widow in those months. Thus, her view of life was shaped and coloured. Of course, like the Queen Mum, she has seen the span of the twentieth century, remembering World War I and the hard times that followed. She came from an age of elegance and grace, style and courtesy, pride and personal duty, dressed in soft-brown and green tweeds, of the sort stitched by her father, who had been a tailor in Glasgow.

The manners of the modern world, with its thrust and ambition, its electronic gadgetry and fevered wheels, were not for my mother. The need for speed didn't encroach on her judgements. Talking was an art and a pleasure, not merely a means of communication.

The night before her death she had been in defiant mood: "They come to my bed with their charts and they say things to each other, but not to me. Perhaps, they think I'm a half-wit, but I'm not a half-wit! I know what's happening."

These thoughts were with us as we sat around her bed in Arrowe Park Hospital, Birkenhead, making small talk. All the staff had been so kind. "The nurses are lovely," my mother said. But the blood was seeping from her aortic rupture. "There's nothing we can do now, we're just keeping her comfortable," said the doctor. "The pain has gone."

My mother understood every word. Hands squeezed under the sheets. Her breathing became slower. And the tea was cooling in the beaker by her bed. I have written all my columns with my mother in mind. I hope more than ever that she likes this one.

WE WILL REMEMBER THEM

THE GREAT WAR

I listened in awe as the old men told me their stories. I felt almost ashamed to be in the company of people who had given so much. And as they spoke in their frailty, I knew that this was their last chance to tell us about what they had seen when their eyes were still young. All are now dead.

The following stories were written to commemorate the 80th anniversary of the Armistice in 1998.

A WAR OF HORRIFYING NUMBERS

In terms of courage and cowardice, stupidity and brilliance, deaths and recruitment, generosity and barbarity, filth and glory, and, most of all, human sacrifice, mankind had never known anything like the Great War. In just over four years, stretching from August 1914 to November 1918, the belligerent nations mobilised 65,038,810 men. Some 8,020,780 were killed in battle and 21,228,813 were wounded. For the first time in history, the civilian dead – 6,642,633 – almost matched the military dead.

In Britain, memories concentrate on the Western Front, the network of trenches which faced each other on a tortuous route from the Swiss border to the Channel coast, but there were other theatres as well for the opposing forces, as they were gradually drawn into the nightmare. On one side were the Allies: France, the British Empire, Russia, Italy, the United States, Belgium, Serbia, Montenegro, Romania, Greece, Portugal, Japan (a total of 42,188,810 people mobilised). On the other, were the Central Powers: Germany, Austria-Hungary, Turkey and Bulgaria (22,850,000 people mobilised).

The German military dead was greatest at 1,808,546; followed by Russia 1,700,000; France 1,357,800; Austria-Hungary 922,500; British Empire 908,371, Italy 462,391; Romania 335,706; Turkey 325,000; Bulgaria 75,844; USA 50,585; Serbia 45,000. Casualties on a smaller scale were suffered by many other nations. The true figures are probably considerably higher than those listed above, which were gathered from estimates, as well as official figures by the compilers of *Jane's Encyclopedia of Military History*.

Of all the terrible names from World War I, the Somme remains the most chilling in the British folk memory. The first battle of the Somme was fought between 24 June and 13 November 1916. After a massive bombardment, the British Army began walking towards the German defences on 1 July. On that day alone, our troops sustained 60,000 casualties, 19,000 of them dead. This was the greatest one-day loss in British military history. By comparison, in World War II, it took 20 days of fighting from the Normandy landings for the combined Anglo/America casualties to reach 60,000.

By the end of the Somme, in which both sides were raked by merciless machine-gun fire, we had lost 420,000 men and the French 195,000. The German loss was estimated at an almost unbelievable 650,000. Only one other battle on the Western Front compared to the Somme. At Verdun, the French lost 542,000. The German casualties were 434,000.

WILF WALLWORTH

The old photograph shows just a boy with a gun. Puttees tight, buttons and buckles polished, he stands proud outside the barracks.

Wilf Wallworth, the gas-lamplighter's son, took the King's shilling and joined the Territorial Army to escape the penury of the cotton mill which blocked the sun from his terraced home in Allstead Street, Oldham. Those days, in the morning before the sun had risen, you could hear the stamp of clogs when the 'shawlie army' was clumping to work with frosted breath and rumbling bellies in towns right across Lancashire's cotton belt. Wilf, as a keen-eyed boy, didn't know it then, but he was soon to see and touch places much worse than those infamous dank, dark, Satanic mills in Blake's Jerusalem. A few weeks later, he joined thousands of other young soldiers facing the Hun at the Third Battle of Ypres. He was 17.

Even by the standards of the Great War, it was a terrible slaughter. The eminent historian, Basil Liddell Hart, was to describe it as, "the last scene in the gloomiest drama in British military history". Wilf, who was seriously wounded during the carnage, remembers the blood, the stench, the fear, the ceaseless noise, and the lice that crawled along his once immaculate uniform. Afterwards, he was to return to the trenches but, despite being twice more wounded, he survived the Great War.

Now he is 100 years old and lives in a nursing home in Liverpool. He keeps his medals and memories, and sometimes at night he hears again the horses scream as their flesh is ripped by enemy bullets and shrapnel.

They talk about the glory of war and of heroes. They were celebrated in the old movies, in the military dispatches, in the newspapers, from the pulpits, and in those places where the air smells clean. Wilf Wallworth and his comrades didn't talk much about the glory when the stench of rotting horse flesh lined their nostrils; when boys, alone in the dark somewhere beyond the barbed wired, cried for their mothers, and everybody heard and nobody came. Ypres, a little market town on the Belgian/French border, was to become a name synonymous with suffering and bravery.

As he sat in his room in the old people's home that had been converted from a former church, Wilf remembered how they had sent him there, when he was a boy of 17, freshly trained by the Territorial Army at Kinmel Bay, North Wales. His memories are not so good on detail now that he is 100, but the mood of that damned battlefield – its smells and fears, the scream of the overhead shell and the barked orders, the taste of the rum and the dryness of the tongue – it all still comes back.

"Eventually they sent me there," he said, in that matter-of-fact way characteristic of so many of those people who lost control of their destiny.

It was July 1917 and the Allies were about to start what the history books were to call the Third Battle of Ypres. Sometimes it was known by a single word with a strange and sorrowful melody in its sound: Passchendaele.

"It was assumed then that we had a battlefront with a row of trenches, then there was the reserve behind you with heavy artillery behind them," said Wilf. "It was nothing like that, of course, but that was how it was supposed to be.

"The Germans, at their nearest, were about two miles from the front line. The closer we were to them, the safer we were, because their shells used to explode and go over the top of us. But when our artillery opened up, we had to send someone back to tell them that they were killing their own men. That's how it worked in those days. The generals only had experience of the Boer War. That's how they were fighting this war.

"Things were so bad that there was nothing but shell-holes, water, dead horses. There were horses lying in rows down there. You could hear them, screaming, as bits were blown off them. There were soldiers with arms off. Shell-shock. I was dragging them in from the enemy shell-holes, from the green water. At night, we used to creep out to get water. You could feel the dead bodies. It would give you a bit of a shock, that kind of thing, but you'd do anything.

"The men in reserve used to bring the rations up. We used to get square biscuits and a bit of cheese. The biscuit was as hard as wood, but it was very acceptable. There were tins of Maconochies." These were tins of thin sliced turnip or carrot in a soup or gravy which, when served cold were known as 'mankillers', but when hot were just about edible. "There were rissoles, and a round cob of bread which had to be cut into four. It had to be exactly equal, because if anyone got a crumb more, then there was a row. We never got no butter or nothing like that. We were starving and we were lousy. We were in the rain all the time. These shells were dropping over, twenty-four hours a day, seven days a week.

"I would be out in No Man's Land, dragging soldiers into shell-holes for safety. I came across a German in a shallow grave, just a few feet deep. He pointed to his foot. His toes had been blown off. I bandaged him up as best I could, but I couldn't do anything with him. I couldn't understand him. All the time this was going on, fellahs were dropping around us."

Wilf was seriously wounded in this incident. As he lay in the mud, hearing the sounds of battle, followed by the screams and moans of men and horses, his voice became dry. "They had given us tots of rum to buck us up before," he said. "The rum made your mouth terribly dry." Eventually, the stretcher-bearers came and ran him to safety. He was treated back in England. Wilf was to be wounded twice more during his service, which was mostly with the Inniskilling Fusiliers.

As he was telling his story in the Woolton Grange Nursing Home, Wilf seemed to find a pattern in the confusion that had taken him from a cobbled street to the grass and mud of Belgium, but interruptions disturbed his recollections and sometimes his thoughts wandered to different places.

This is the way it is for him. There are these images of Hell, sometimes fading from view, but all true, much truer than the listing of events in chronological order, as they do in the books. Wilf is not talking about victories and defeats. No heavenly strings were plucked over the soldiers dying at Ypres. This wasn't Hollywood where boys rise into Heaven clasping a locket holding the face of a sweetheart at home.

"When we were going out for a rest, we were all in a shocking state," he continued. "We were hungry and tired. We used to take our pants off and run a match or a candle up the seams to kill the lice. Then we would have a big fire and get hot water. We would take all our clothes off, put them in a big net bag and fumigate them and we'd have a shower. A couple of days later, you were just as lousy as ever again. That was one of the difficulties."

A useful tip for the soldiers, he said, was to land on your back if you slipped on the slime of the duckboards that ran down the trenches. Those who fell on their faces were likely to suffocate, or catch a deadly disease from the filthy water and mud. These were the lessons quickly learnt by the young Wilf.

In some ways, joining the army was the escape he had yearned for when he gazed from his bedroom window at the gasworks that employed his father John, and at the mill where he and his mother Emma worked.

"There was no dole then. You either worked or you starved," said Wilf. "I started at the mill when I was twelve years of age. I was a half-timer. You could work at twelve if you had enough attendances at school. At thirteen, you had to leave school, whether you wanted to or not. You used to get three shillings and threepence a week in the mill (about seventeen pence)."

At a quarter past four every morning, the knocker-up rapped on the doors with his bamboo cane, so that the occupants wouldn't be late for work. On Saturday mornings, Wilf earned a few coppers more by lathering the faces of customers awaiting a shave in the barber's shop. From his wages, he was allowed three old pence to spend. It bought a ticket to the cinema, two Woodbines and a savoury-filled muffin.

Then someone suggested that he should join the Territorials. You had to be 5ft 3in with a chest measurement of 33in. If you were accepted, you could go to camp for two weeks. "That's a good idea, I thought," said Wilf. He was rejected first time, but the second time, he was in. "They gave me a shilling for signing up," he said.

In civilian life, Wilf, who out-lived his wives Nellie and Edith, was a plumber, a painter and a signwriter. He had no children. His war service was recognised with three service medals, but of late, Wilf has become something of a celebrity, receiving telegrams from the Queen and certificates marking his age and experience. One made him an honorary member of The 1st Battalion, The Royal Irish Regiment. It reads:

4944 Lance Corporal Wilfred Wallworth celebrated his 100th birthday on July 27 1998. Lcpl Wallworth was a serving member of the Inniskillings. During his service defending our great Nation in the War to End all Wars. He was wounded three times. In recognition of his former military service.

FREDERICK FYFE, PHOTOGRAPHER

They have no smell and they have no touch, but these lights and shadows will soon be all that is left of those deadly theatres where the curtains were held open for the four years of World War I. Now, wars are filmed almost routinely and families spoon their TV dinners as the pictures of starvation and suffering fill the screen. But then, the images from the trenches, now ghosts cradled in sepia shades and curled corners, gave civilians a hint of the terrible sacrifices being made by the soldiers of the Great War. The men who took the photographs, which gave some of the soldiers this strange immortality, were themselves heroes.

Foremost among them was Frederick Alexander Fyfe of Liverpool, who was a soldier with a camera, rather than a photographer in a uniform. It was that closeness with comrades-in-arms which was to make his record of the attacks and the retreats, the bravery and the fear, such a compelling record.

Private 1600 Fyfe joined the 10th Scottish Battalion of the King's Regiment (Liverpool) and was part of the British Expeditionary Force, which fought in the First Battle of Ypres. Fifty years later, he was to revisit the scenes where his brave comrades, dismissed by the bellicose Kaiser Wilhelm II as the 'Old Contemptibles', had suffered such dreadful losses.

He sat, an old man, on the veranda of the restaurant in the restored majesty of the Grand Palace at Ypres, near the graves of the young. The carillon of the restored Cloth Hall was pealing sad music. It had been a smouldering ruin when last he had seen it, while shuffling along on the cobbles of the Menin Road, with the blood from a bullet hole trickling down his right leg. He was one of the men wounded on 16 June 1916, while assaulting the Bellewaarde Ridge during the Battle of Hooge, the saddest day in the proud history of the Liverpool Scottish, now recorded simply as Hooge Day. His leg had gone all "goosey", he said. Nevertheless, as he lay in No Man's Land at half past four in the morning, Fyfe managed to take pictures of the slaughter as the shells from big-calibre guns exploded around him. The negatives were concealed in a pouch of his bandolier and later published in British newspapers.

In that single engagement, Fyfe saw the flower of his comrades scythed down by German guns. AM McGilchrist was to record it in his book, *Liverpool Scottish 1900 to 1919* (published in Liverpool by Henry Young and Sons in 1930): Four officers and 75 other ranks were killed, 11 officers and 201 other ranks wounded, six officers and 103 other ranks missing. Of the missing, all the officers and, with a very few exceptions, all the men, were subsequently reported killed. The Liverpool Scottish had practically ceased to exist. They had definitely proved themselves as a fighting unit and set the seal to their previous record in the brigade.

Several excellent photographs are extant which were actually taken during the action. Private Fyfe, Z Company, who was wounded very shortly after the engagement began, thought that he might usefully employ his time until the stretcher bearers came for him and, taking from one of his pouches his best pocket camera, he obtained very good snapshots of the ground between the British and German trenches and the supports coming up.

It is hardly necessary to say that there were orders strictly prohibiting the carrying of cameras, and there was serious trouble in store for the man found in possession of one. Perhaps the fact that Fyfe is by profession a press photographer, makes some excuse for him having overlooked this embarrassing order.

Fyfe later explained how he had emptied two pockets from his bandolier, so that he could hide the film. "I only carried thirty bullets instead of fifty," he said, "but I think I can be forgiven, because I got the pictures that showed the people back home what the war was like.

"My camera was a tiny German Goerz, about the size of a packet of twenty cigarettes. It used glass plates less than two inches square. I had used it in Liverpool to take pictures of the Assize courts in St George's Hall." Other soldiers had smuggled the plates to him as cough lozenges.

Fyfe, who was to be commissioned as a lieutenant, was awarded the Military Cross for his deeds at Givenchy during the battle of the Somme in 1916. His citation read:

For conspicuous bravery when in command of a raiding party. The party were discovered at the enemy's wires, and a heavy fire opened to them. He threw several bombs into their trench, and, after remaining behind until his party had been withdrawn, made a gallant attempt to bring in one of his wounded men.

Later, Fyfe was to join the Royal Flying Corps (forerunner of the RAF) and claimed at least three German aircraft during dog fights.

After the war, Fyfe was to work with distinction as a freelance photographer on Merseyside, many of his pictures appearing in the *Daily Post*. In World War II, he served with the RAF as a squadron leader. During the Battle of the Atlantic he was in charge of photography at Liverpool's Derby House, headquarters of Western Approaches Command.

Fred Fyfe lived in Huyton. He died in 1971, aged 82. Shortly before his death, he came to the aid of a bus conductress being threatened by two young thugs who had refused to pay their fares. They retreated before the swings of his steel walking stick.

TED RIMMER

It was the autumn of 1918 and the boys and men were mustering at Southport railway station beneath the spreading steam of a troop train. Young Ted Rimmer felt a new strength in his mother's hug. Never before had they held each other so close. No words were needed because they sensed that this hug, on the cold stone, was their last goodbye.

But a few weeks later, as the strangest quiet ever heard cloaked the trenches and the naked woods, Ted began a letter to his mother, Elizabeth: *Dear Mum, the war is over, I'll be coming home shortly. I am safe.*

Eighty years after the Great War's Armistice, those simple words, scribbled on an Army-issue card, from a son to his mother, carry an eternal message of love and faith. So the mother and son were reunited.

That was a long time ago. Today Ted is celebrating his 100th birthday party and you could open a mint with all the medals polished on the chests of the friends and retired servicemen lining up to shake his hand; a hand with strong bones and the long veins of experience.

Rifleman 88251, the only World War I veteran left from the Liverpool King's Regiment, was surrounded by those who loved him personally and respected him for what he did on the faraway meadows of France. Sitting at a table, Ted spoke of his experiences as a 19-year-old in the Third Battle of Ypres, known as Passchendaele.

"I remember going down the duckboards and it was frozen. Then I fell through the ice into a shell-hole. It was full of dead men. They had been there for months. It stank. It was terrible. All this time, the shelling was going on and I was up to here," he said, pointing high. "I would have drowned, but I was pulled out by the officer and he gave me a drink from a flask of rum. But I still had to go on and I was in a front line shell-hole for a week after that, and I never even got a cold."

Sitting in a wheelchair near Ted was his 95-year-old wife, Nell, and her nurse from the home where she now lives. Ted, his eyes a little moist, rose from his chair and with the help of his stick, walked towards Nell, watched by his son Gerry and his wife Anne. He kissed her full on the lips, like he did when they were young and, for a few minutes, they sat together again and Ted stroked Nell's right arm. The couple and their friends were in the Merseyside Police Club, Fairfield, because he joined the force after the war.

In the corridor, between the bar and the assembly room where the speeches were to be made, standard-bearers Tom Christian, Eric Ponting, Robert Draper, Danny Duffy, Eric Collings and Harold White were forming a guard of honour. They represented organisations including the Normandy Veterans' Association, the France and German Cross Association, the Merseyside branch of the Royal Artillery, the Liverpool Royal British Legion, the 7th Ghurka Regiment, the Queen's Lancashire Regiment, the Royal Naval Association, the 8th Irish Battalion, the King's Regiment, the Bedfordshire and Hertfordshire Regiment, the Palestine Police and the Middle East Forces.

As Ted walked into the room and smiled, the 14-strong Merseyside Police Band, led by PC Mal Peters, struck up *On the Square*. All 70 men and women stood and clapped in rhythm. Liverpool Lord Mayor Bert Herrity, Distinguished Flying Cross, opened the formal proceedings by presenting the old man with a telegram from the Queen, another from the people of Liverpool and a bottle of champagne. Merseyside Assistant Chief Constable Paul Acres, representing Chief Constable Sir James Sharples, said: "It is a great privilege to meet a man who has done so very much over a long and distinguished lifetime."

Turning to the centenarian, who had dressed in a smart brown suit with six gleaming medals, Mr Acres added: "I can only read with fascination, pride and humility about some of the things you have done."

Ted was born in Southport and educated at the local Linacre Street School, before he joined Smith's booksellers in 1912. Four years later, he enlisted with the King's 2nd Liverpool Rifles. Mr Acres said: "He was a sniper/scout who went out into a No Man's Land seeking a way forward for colleagues raiding enemy trenches. The survival rates in the Great War were pretty low anyway. It was phenomenal for people performing deeds such as Ted, to get through the war at all."

From the floor, Ted took the microphone to tell a story which happened during the Allied advance into the Hindenberg Line in the closing weeks of the war.

"With a colleague I went down to a dug-out and it was furnished like a proper room. There was a bottle of wine on the table. This colleague of mine said 'Oh, we'll have that' and he took it upstairs. Then he took the cork out and it exploded. It had been booby-trapped and all his insides were blown out. He died. I could have picked up that bottle."

Later, tributes were paid to Ted's service as a policeman. He joined the force in 1919 during the Liverpool Police Strike that resulted in 906 officers being sacked after widespread looting. He left the police in 1951, but from 1953 until 1968 he was manager of the Allerton Police Station canteen. When these tributes were finished, the band began playing and the Kingsman offered his arm to his daughter-in-law, Anne. Together, they danced as their friends clapped in affection and admiration.

Before the excellent buffet was served and the whisky glasses raised, Ted cleared his throat and remembered the song sung in the trenches. "If you want the sergeant-major, I know where he is, I know where he is … I saw him, I saw him, hanging on the old barbed wire." Ted, like so many thousands of young men, had been caught in the barbed wire as he advanced on enemy positions, but he was able to rip himself free from what would otherwise have been sure death.

"I never expected all this," said Ted who lives an independent life at his home in Broadgreen. "It has come as a great surprise to me, the Lord Mayor and the assistant chief constable being here. I'm a person of no importance."

As those around him shook their heads, Ted's thoughts returned to the war. "You know that comrade on the Hindenberg Line. When he lay on the ground with all his stomach out, he opened his eyes and looked at me and said 'Mother' and then he was dead."

Ted Rimmer was outside Arras in Northern France when the Armistice broke. He remembers: "I couldn't get over the silence. There were no shells, you know. The Germans had been sending over these high velocity shells. You couldn't hear them until they came close to you. But after eleven am, there was this complete silence. The first thing I thought was that I should send a letter to my mother because I was the only one and she was terrified of me getting killed. We all stood around. I thought how lucky we were really – well I thought we were – because out of all the millions who had gone, I was never killed or even hit by a shell or a bullet. It was amazing. I wrote on the card, 'The war is over, Mum. I'll be coming home shortly. I am safe'. We were very close."

SOME THINGS STAY JUST THE SAME

Gathered at the Museum of Liverpool Life, on the Mersey waterfront, for the opening of an exhibition called, 'We Will Remember Them' were: Ted Rimmer, 100, of the Liverpool King's Regiment; Wilf Wallworth, 100, of Liverpool King's Regiment; Edward Brown, 102, the only surviving member of the Liverpool Old Pals; and Dick Trafford, 99, who joined the Liverpool King's Regiment before being transferred to the Machine Gun Corps.

Dick Trafford was brushing his trilby with the stump of his left thumb – it had been sliced off by a fragment of shell at the Somme. Above it, were his medals for gallantry. For him, the Armistice anniversary brought back mixed memories. He said: "I hadn't eaten for three days. Our advance guard was chasing the German rearguard. Then we got word that the Armistice was going to be the next day.

"At eleven am we were sat down on the road next to one another. There was not a word out of us. It could have been pancake Tuesday for all we cared. We were too tired.

"Then, the day after, in a village in Belgium, an old chap pointed to a bakehouse where they were making bread. So there was a rush of the troops to the bakehouse. I don't know who paid for the bread. But at least we had something to eat."

The ceremony began with a minute's silence, after which Ted Rimmer laid a wreath of poppies before a case containing plaster-cast figures of soldiers in action. They were sculpted by Sir William Goscombe John as the moulds for the War Memorial in Port Sunlight Village, unveiled in 1921. Behind Ted, standing so still that at first they looked like exhibits, were two of today's Kingsmen, dressed in black pith helmets with spikes and scarlet tunics similar to those used in the film, *Zulu*. Their bugles played the *Last Post* and the *Reveille,* to begin and end the silence. It was a gesture of continuity from the young to the old, and the shine from the medals, buckles and buttons of today reached down a long parade of triumph and grief.

Drum Major Gary Copland and Kingsman Edward Wood wore sashes into which were embroidered the names of many great battles fought by their regimental predecessors. These included Loos, Mons, Marne, Somme, Piave and Cambrai from the Great War. The carnage enclosed in those names is unimaginable to the civilians of this generation, but still the killing goes on. Above Gary's left breast were three silver medals, two awarded for tours of duty in Northern Ireland, and the third for 15 years of good conduct in the Army.

Kingsman Wood is just 20, an age beyond the dreams of so many men in the trenches. He said: "Everybody remembers the men who risked their lives and died to save their country. It is great to see some of the survivors here today.

"You know, it's curious, but there are things that are exactly the same, whether you are talking about World War One, World War Two, or any conflict the Army has ever been in to this day," said Major Copland. "You can imagine, in the trenches, people being told when the shells were coming in, 'You haven't shaved this morning'. You would look at the sergeant major as if to say, 'I might be dead in half-an-hour' and then I think, 'Hang about, that's happened to me in the past'.

"You always have the sergeant major, it doesn't matter what war you are in. You have just had an adrenaline rush, you have just had a fight, hand to hand, a close quarters battle. You're in there, you've done the business, you're sitting there having a cigarette and thinking you're brilliant, and then the company sergeant major brings you right back down to earth by saying, 'Put that cigarette out, face that way and get yourself into a firing position. Who the Hell do you think you are?' Every soldier from the old men here today will tell you exactly the same. You think you're the bee's knees, but the sergeant major will tell you who the boss is. That's why we are the best army in the world.

"It won't be long before there are no First World War veterans left to talk to. They are all very old blokes, it's going to be a shame, but we must never forget them. I will make sure that my young lad (Gary, aged seven) knows about it and hears some of the stories that I have been told."

Thus, their past becomes our future.

HAROLD ANDERSON

He was the last one. Harold Anderson, teenage soldier and drummer from a battalion almost destroyed in World War I, died at the age of 102, just weeks before he would have received the Légion d'Honneur, one of the highest French awards for gallantry. Friends and family of Private Anderson of the Liverpool Scottish will be gathering for his funeral at exactly the moment the guns fell silent on the Western Front 80 years ago: the 11th hour of the 11th day of the 11th month, the three elevens that mark the Armistice. A piper and a drummer from the Liverpool Scottish will play his coffin into the brick chapel at Landican Cemetery, Birkenhead, and as the curtains close over the crematorium, the piper will sound him out with a dirge.

In 1914, on 1 November, Private Anderson crossed the Channel with the other members of the 10th Scottish Battalion of the King's (Liverpool) Regiment, and headed for the battlefields. He had joined the Territorials just two years earlier. The old boy from the Blue Coat School, Wavertree, somehow survived the carnage of numerous engagements.

He was just a fresh-faced volunteer serving in the stores behind the lines during the Battle of Hooge on 16 June 1915 when the Liverpool Scottish was almost wiped out by German machine-gun fire. The sorrowful day is recorded in history simply as Hooge day. It is known that he had seen action in several battles and that he had also been a drummer, but, in common with many Great War veterans, Mr Anderson, who was promoted to Lance Corporal, was reluctant to tell his friends and family at home about what he had seen. Even the news that he was to receive the Légion d'Honneur was received with equanimity by Mr Anderson. The news had arrived just days before his death.

"He was very, very laid back," said his daughter Phyllis Rucinski, "and he asked if there would be a small pension with it. He was with the Territorials on the outbreak of war and he was mobilised immediately. They were put in the old Shakespeare Theatre, Liverpool, and shipped straight out to France."

Immediately after the war, Phyllis explained, Mr Anderson couldn't find work in England. He went to sea on a liner as a waiter before working in Canada, where he saved enough money to pay the fare over for a girl whom he had met while on leave from France.

His sweetheart, Winifred Parker, travelled to Canada and that Saturday they married in a little Scottish Presbyterian church in Montreal. They were there for more than nine years before returning to the UK, where they eventually established the Anderson's bakery shop in St Paul's Road, Seacombe, Wallasey. The couple had three children: Phyllis, Buddy (who died three years ago), and Gordon, who lives in New Zealand. Winifred died in 1990, aged 91.

To Phyllis, Mr Anderson wasn't just a hero of the Great War, he was her father.

"My father and mother were wonderful parents," she said. "They gave us such a happy childhood. I couldn't fault them, they were just wonderful. He was always there to help you. He was a wonderful father."

Mr Anderson died peacefully at the Anchorage old people's home, Hoylake, just days after receiving the invitation to the award ceremony. He had been very happy at the Anchorage, and was regularly visited by Phyllis.

The special ceremony will be held at the London Library. Eighty years after the Great War's Armistice, the frail remnant of the 8,904,467 men mobilised by the British Empire are to have pinned on their old, proud chests, medals that will speak forever of their bravery, and of the sacrifice made by their comrades who never returned.

Never before in the history of man will so many centenarians – some supported by sticks, others in wheelchairs, all borne by memory – have been saluted by a foreign power. Great War veterans will each receive a Légion d'Honneur medal from the French Military attaché, Colonel Michel Perrodon. Medals will be sent to the homes of those unfit to travel.

The trip is being organised by the chairman of the World War I Veterans' Association (Liverpool Branch), John Patterson, who is also the deputy head of Ranworth Square Primary School, Norris Green. He said: "We should always remember people who were apart from their loved ones. These men put so much into their country and received nothing back. We should always be grateful for what they did and remember them for what they went through. If you ever talk or spend any time with these men, you'd feel just the same."

A spokesman for the Royal British Legion said: "This is the last chance that we will have this century to honour a group of people who remain with us, who had the most sterling of attitudes and did the most amazing things, and it is good that the French have decided to award them the Légion d' Honneur," the spokesman said.

Survivors from Merseyside who will either collect or be sent the medal include: Ted Rimmer, aged 100, of the King's Regiment, Wilf Wallworth, 100, of the Royal Irish Regiment; Herman Smithers, 101, of the Royal Engineers, Edward Brown, 102, the only surviving Liverpool Pal; Dick Trafford, 99, of the King's (Liverpool) Regiment and later the Machine Gun Corps; Bob Taylor, 100, of the South Lancs Regiment; and Leo McCormack, 101, of the Field Artillery.

Although the intention was to decorate survivors only, Mr Anderson's medal had already been agreed by the French authorities and the spokesman for the Royal British Legion said that meant the posthumous award would be given to his family.

At Harold's funeral service and cremation at Landican Cemetery, Birkenhead. Rev Elaine Chegwin Hall, said: "It would have been entirely appropriate for Harold to have received the medal from the French Government, had he lived just a little while longer. Yet his time had come and we honour him now in our hearts and minds for his memory, his contribution to our lives and to the lives of those no longer here."

THE SIGNIFICANCE OF THE POPPY

Millions of young people on the streets today reach for the memory of their forefathers by wearing a simple flower fashioned from pressed paper with a black plastic stud as its pod.

The seeds in the pod once offered a doomed generation faith that life would be renewed in those naked fields and woods where all else lay broken and still. Such was the devastation of Flanders and Picardy in Northern France, seen by the fresh-eyed sons who came and fell and bled in their tens of thousands, joining those who had fallen before them. To them, it seemed that nothing but the poppy could live in that stained mud. Its blooming, deep crimson, with the warm weather, opened a glimpse of tomorrow.

John McCrea, a doctor serving with the Canadian Armed Forces, was so appalled by the scene, that in 1915 he scribbled a few lines in his pocket book:

> In Flanders' fields the poppies blow
> Between the crosses row on row,
> That marks our place: and in the sky
> The larks, still bravely singing, fly
> Scarce heard amid the guns below.

This opening verse and the rest of McCrea's poem was published in *Punch* magazine as *In Flanders' Fields*. Soon after the war finished, it was read by Moina Michael, an American War Secretary with the YMCA in Paris. From the sorrow she felt in the message, she wrote her own memorial verse:

> And now the torch and Poppy red
> Wear in honour of our dead.

Miss Michael bought poppies with money that had been given to her by colleagues and, wearing one of the poppies that she had bought, sold the others to friends to raise some money for servicemen in need. A French colleague, Madame Guerin, encouraged by what Miss Michael had achieved with this simple symbol, proposed the selling of artificial poppies to help ex-servicemen and their dependants. So the movement started in France, which was then mourning the deaths of 1,357,000 servicemen.

Across the Channel in Britain, Major George Howson, a young infantry officer who had been decorated for gallantry, was also deeply concerned about the plight of the war disabled who seemed unemployable in peacetime Britain. He formed the Disabled Society to help them. Meanwhile, Field Marshal Earl Douglas Haig, formerly the Commander-in-Chief in France, had formed the Royal British Legion to give practical help and companionship to the ex-service men and women and their dependants. The British Empire had lost 908,371 men in the war. The first Poppy Day was held in this country on 11 November 1921, and it was a great success.

Although its deepest association is with the Great War, the poppy has grown into the symbol of sacrifices made by the British military in all subsequent conflicts from the Second World War to Bosnia and Rwanda. The poppies are made by 120 disabled serviceman at the Legion's factory in Richmond, Surrey. More than 32 million lapel poppies a year, 100,000 wreaths and 400,000 Remembrance Crosses are ordered each year. Last year's Poppy Appeal raised more than £17m.

The money is used to pay for the 450 ex-servicemen living in the Legion's residential homes and for the 4000 needing convalescent care annually. Welfare services, like hospital visits and meal deliveries, are carried out by 2,500 caseworkers. A special department deals with 60,000 war disability pension inquires a year. Another department helps those leaving the services develop good civilian lives. The Legion helps widows visit cemeteries in the 40 different countries where their husbands were buried. The Legion has 700,142 members, including 89,500 in the Women's Section. Of its 3,180 branches, 78 are overseas. The women's section has 1,610 branches. It has 886 clubs.

Three years after writing the poem, John McCrea died in a military hospital on the French Channel coast. Soldiers looking from their windows could see the British coast rising from the sea. In the moments before his death, McCrea whispered some words from the last verse of his poem:

If ye break faith with us who died
We shall not sleep, though poppies grow
In Flanders' Fields.

WILFRED OWEN

There is one grave among the millions. It looks just like all the others, white and mute in the green grass, but a voice rises still from the frail figure lying there, with the half smile of infinite bewilderment. It speaks for all the young men who would never again dance, dress a Christmas tree, or see their children grow tall and strong. It is the voice from the blasted meadows of France and it will carry, from the cold places where birdsong once died, to those people who care to remember; always.

Wilfred Owen, son and brother, soldier and hero, but most of all poet, died 80 years ago, exactly a week before the Armistice. With the concern for others, which so characterised his bravery, Owen was shepherding his men across the Sambre

Canal, near the little town of Ors, against heavy German machine-gun fire. It wasn't one of the great engagements of the war, but comrades saw Lieutenant Owen moving among his men, encouraging them in yet another advance which they hoped would end the slaughter.

He fell, as so many had done before him, bleeding from a bullet fired by a stranger in the quick-passing fever of another little hell.

A few weeks earlier, Owen had completed what many were to regard as his finest poem with the lines:

> *I am the enemy you killed, my friend.*
> *I knew you in this dark: for so you frowned*
> *Yesterday through me as you jabbed and killed.*
> *I parried; but my hands were loath and cold.*
> *Let us sleep now...*

Strange Meeting, along with *Anthem for Doomed Youth*, *Greater Love* and *Spring Offensive*, are among the poems that Owen offered the world in support of his much-quoted purpose: "My subject is war and the pity of war. The poetry is in the pity."

At the time of his death, Owen had no public beyond his family and a dedicated coterie of writers. Most of his poems existed only in fragments, which were painstakingly gathered by fellow poet, Siegfried Sassoon. And, later, Jon Stallworthy, who was to edit a complete volume of his work. Just five poems were published in his lifetime. They were *Song of Songs*, *The Next War*, *Miners*, *Futility* and *Hospital Barge*.

Owen's posthumous reputation began in 1920 when Sassoon published 23 of his poems. That raised his place high in the pantheon of war poets and it was to be sustained through the troubled decades ahead which, of course, embraced another terrible war. In 1962, Owen was introduced to a new peace-seeking generation when some of his poems were included in Benjamin Britten's *War Requiem*.

Once confronted with the terror and stench of the trenches, Owen heard his poetic calling, but that has not prevented special-interest parties from claiming him as their own. The broader Labour movement have represented him as the common man's poet, noting that his background lacked the privilege associated with contemporaries such as Rupert Brooke, Laurence Binyon and Siegfried Sassoon. Homosexual sympathies were excited by the close, almost fatherly, friendship Sassoon held for Owen. Peace campaigners read his poems as an outright condemnation of war. There is something in all three, but none has the monopoly.

Wilfred Edward Salter Owen was born to Tom and Susan on 18 March 1893 in Plas Wilmot, a large red-bricked house on the outskirts of Oswestry owned by Susan's father, Alderman Edward Shaw, a former mayor of the town. A substantial part of their family ironmongery capital had already been devoured by Susan's brother, Edward, who gambled heavily and enjoyed a drink. The house was sold on the Alderman's death in 1897 and Tom Owen was appointed to a supervisory post in Birkenhead with the Great Western and London and North East Railways. Later that year, he moved to another railway job in Shrewsbury, where Wilfred's brother Harold was born. In 1898, Tom brought his wife and three children to Birkenhead, where he had been made stationmaster at Woodside Station, near the ferry terminal.

The family settled in Birkenhead and Wilfred was enrolled at Birkenhead Institute, which then served the sons of merchants with a strong rudimentary education. His burgeoning talents were to win him several prizes. Doting mother Susan would have been relieved to see her son at a school of some local standing as she was determined to raise her children in genteel circumstances despite her husband's comparatively modest income. Their houses in Willmer Road, Elm Grove and Milton Street, suggested a lower middle-class respectability, where white collars hid empty purses and stews simmered on the hearth.

It was with some relief that the parents and their children, Wilfred, Mary, Harold and Colin, returned to Shrewsbury. Tom had been appointed Assistant Superintendent with the GW and LNER, Western Region. After leaving the Shrewsbury Technical School, Wilfred worked in an unpaid capacity for the Rev Herbert Wigan at his parish in Dunsden, before entering a series of private tutorial posts, finally teaching English in Bordeaux.

He enlisted with the Artists' Rifles in October 1915 and was commissioned as a second lieutenant into the Manchester Regiment, but it was not until January 1917 that he was to see action as the commander of a platoon.

In a letter home, the somewhat arrogant Owen bemoans his lack of experience and mocks his juvenile interest in the romantic poets: "What does Keats have to teach me of rifle and machine-gun drill? How will my pass in botany teach me to lunge a bayonet? How will Shelley show me how to hate, or any poet teach me the trajectory of a bullet?" In the coming weeks, Owen was to learn a lot about all those things which by then belonged to the common understanding of the soldier.

Although he is remembered as a poet, Owen was also a robust prose writer. Writing home from a hospital on the Somme, where he was being treated for concussion, he wrote home:

Already I have comprehended a light which will never filter into the dogma of any national church: namely that one of Christ's essential commands was: "Passivity at any price! Suffer dishonour and disgrace but never resort to arms. Be bullied, be outraged, be killed: but do not kill". It may be a chimerical and an ignominious principle, but there it is ... And I am not myself a conscientious objector with a very seared conscience.

To his brother, Harold, he described an assault in an enemy trench:

The sensations of going over the top are about as exhilarating as those dreams of falling over a precipice, when you see the rocks at the bottom surging up to you. I awoke without being squashed. Some didn't.

In his poem *Spring Offensive*, Owen expressed similar sentiments:

> *So, soon they topped the hill, and raced together*
> *Over an open stretch of herb and heather*
> *Exposed. And instantly the whole sky burned*
> *With fury against them; earth set sudden cups*
> *In thousands for their blood; and the green slope*
> *Chasmed and deepened sheer to infinite space.*

After his treatment for neurasthenia in Craiglockhart War Hospital, near Edinburgh, where he had his momentous meeting with Sassoon, Owen returned to the trenches. In December, he was promoted to lieutenant. In October, he was awarded the Military Cross, the second highest award for courage in action. His citation read:

> *For conspicuous gallantry and devotion to duty in the attack on the Fonsomme Line on October 12th .*
> *On their company commander becoming a casualty, he assumed command and showed fine leadership and resisted a heavy counter-attack. He personally manipulated a captured enemy machine-gun from an isolated position and inflicted considerable losses on the enemy. Throughout, he behaved most gallantly.*

Then came the assault on the Sambre Canal.

As the church bells pealed peace on 11 November, there was a knock on the door of the Owen family's three-storey, semi-detached home, Machim, in Monkmoor Road, Shrewsbury. It was the telegram …

Wilfred Owen's grave is the third in from the left end of the back row in the cemetery's special enclosure for the war dead. Over him stands a simple white marble headstone with the words: *WES Owen, MC Manchester Regiment. 4th November 1918 Age 25.* Fresh flowers are laid by him almost every day.

> *What passing-bells for these who die as cattle?*
> *Only the monstrous anger of the guns.*
> *Only the stuttering rifles' rapid rattle*
> *Can patter out their hasty orisons …*

AFTER THE WAR

It was meant to be a fit country for heroes to live in, but the fine words of Prime Minister David Lloyd George brought scant comfort to the men in the long queue, hoping there would be enough soup left in the great urn to fill their cans. If not, they would have to make do with a dollop of red jam spooned from a seven pound jar and smeared over a hunk of bread – again.

At night, these men huddled together under their coats just as they had on the battlefields of France and Belgium. Then, they were heroes. Now, they were in huts, fashioned from leaves, branches and rags, on Bidston Hill, overlooking the idle docks of Birkenhead. This was the hungry thirties. Yet there was something each man feared more than starvation, disease, even war. To be buried in a pauper's grave, unmarked, unsung, and un-mourned, was a terrible shame. It was as though you had never been here.

They expressed this fear as they waited for their food in the line leading to the British Legion's building on the edge of Birkenhead Park. Their comrades, who had not fallen on such hard times, decided to start a fund to buy plots where poor war veterans could be buried. It was a long way from the speech made by Lloyd George after the Armistice. "What is our task?" he asked. "To make Britain a fit country for heroes to live in." In those days, a basic funeral cost about £10. The dole was nine shillings (45p) a week and a labourer earned about £1.50 a week.

In all, 65 men were buried in Landican and Flaybrick cemeteries. The funeral ceremonies were simple and there were no headstones. Often several men occupied each plot. But the cemetery authorities recorded the name, the address (where applicable), the age and the place and date of burial of each man. The last man was buried in a Legion plot in 1950.

When they were checking their records recently, Reg Bell, branch chairman, and George Rose, its welfare office, came across the deeds for the burial plots. It was decided that name-markers should be placed over the graves. Now, with another fund, and the help of Wirral Borough Council, the Legion is finishing this job. When it is done, a special commemorative service will be held for all 69 World War I veterans who died too poor to pay for their own burials.

Birkenhead played an important part in the creation of the Legion. As a port, where civilian jobs were often scarce, the town has always produced a large number of soldiers and sailors. After the First World War, it was full of veterans, many with missing limbs or shell-shock. Some joined comrades' groups which met in pubs and halls. They were running into the slump that resulted in the General Strike of 1926 and the hunger marches.

Among these men was Frederick Lister, who had served as a lance-bombardier in France. With the influential help and advice of Earl Haig, commander-in-chief on the Western Front, Lister formed the British Legion from the National Association of Discharged Sailors and Soldiers, the National Federation of Discharged and Demobilised Sailors and Soldiers, Comrades of the Great War, and the Officers' Association. Birkenhead was one of the Legion's founding branches and was opened on 7 July 1921. Mr Lister was on the committee and he was also the national chairman. In 1961, he was knighted for his services to the Legion. He died five years later, aged 79.

Now George Rose is bending over the grass at Landican Cemetery to press a marker into the wet earth.

"The men came back from the trenches to dreadful conditions," he said. "You were lucky to have an outside toilet for six people in some of the buildings in Birkenhead. The buildings were put up strictly for the labourers on the docks. They were little more than cattle houses. Many people were out of work. The shipyards collapsed after the war.

"If you look at the death certificates of most of these men, you will find that most died from pneumonia, which really meant they had died from their living conditions. Even so, people would do anything rather than go into a pauper's grave. That is why the men in the Legion started buying the plots – so the men wouldn't suffer that final indignity. Now we have markers for them and we are planning a service for relatives of all the men."

The men were all from the Birkenhead area and twenty of them were homeless at the time of death.

WORLD WAR II

They said it would never happen again after the slaughter in the trenches, but 19 years later we were at war again. Like all wars, it was the story of butchers and saints, brave men and fools. It was my privilege to speak to some of the men and women who were there.

THE NORWEGIAN SEAFARERS

They were tough young men in the thick woollen pullovers of home. Already, their freshly-shaved faces had been salted by the sea spray once known to their ancestors, men whose dragon-headed longboats explored the coasts of distant lands.

It is 9 April 1940, and the sailors in ports, rivers and seas all over the world, are listening to the wireless broadcasts which tell of how Norway has been invaded by the Germans, and the resistance was collapsing.

There was a choice before the young men now. They could continue the struggle from their ships, or they could slink back home to an occupied country under the leadership of Hitler's puppet Vidkun Quisling, the man who gave his name to shame. Germany celebrated the seizure of Norway as another flash of Hitlerian genius. Newspapers recorded how Britain and France had entered Norwegian waters to lay mines which were intended to prevent the little country trading with Germany.

Most decided to fight for a free Norway, wherever that fight might take them. About 1000 ships that had been with the Royal Navy of Norway, or its Merchant Navy, joined the Allied war effort under the flag of Nortraship (the Norwegian Shipping and Trading Mission) set up 13 days after the invasion. By the end of the war, 570 of those ships had been destroyed by enemy action with the loss of some 4,500 lives. In all, 25,000 Norwegian seamen joined the Allies. Many journeyed to Liverpool, where they were to join the Atlantic convoys carrying supplies to the Soviet Union. With the Norwegian Government and Royal Family in exile in London, friendship was strengthened between the two seafaring nations.

To the Blitz-weary girls on the Home Front, the prospect of romance with a handsome Viking would have seemed like something from the movies, but here they were in the flesh. So, on Sunday mornings, the girls headed for the country with a picnic basket for two on one arm and a blond sailor on the other. Soon, they were dancing cheek-to-cheek as the big bands played in the shimmering halls on both sides of the Mersey.

Hundreds of the sailors married, adding to the small Norwegian community already settled on Merseyside. Others died in the freezing sea as they faced attacks from U-boats and aircraft while carrying cargoes of fuel, oil and munitions to Murmansk. The survivors formed a 'colony' on Merseyside, which met at the Norwegian Church in Southwood Road, St Michael's Hamlet, but it closed in 1992. Then they joined the larger congregation at the Swedish Church on Park Lane, a distinctive, late-Victorian building overlooking the south docks. This was a reversal of their international status, Norway having gained its independence from Sweden in 1905.

Kristian Hansen was on the oil tanker *Pan Norway* which was pulling into the Panama Canal on 9 April when news of the invasion broke. At times like that, first, you think of your family and friends. Then you think of the wider picture. "We were mad about it," said Kristian, now aged 78, "but we didn't think that our small country would be able to resist for long against the Germans."

He came to Liverpool in 1941 and served on the Atlantic convoys. In 1946, Kristian met Edith Swanick at a Saturday night dance in St Luke's Church Hall, Wallasey. "We were sitting around like wallflowers waiting for someone to ask us to dance and he came up to me," she said. "He was the first Norwegian I have ever spoken to in my life."

Harry Jurgensen was enjoying a drinking session at the Del Monica in Cape Town when the news came. "There were three of us in the restaurant," he recalled. "We were shocked. We didn't know what to do before we went back to the ship and the captain gave the instructions. We could go back to Norway and be under the Germans, or sail with Nortraship for a free Norway. Like the majority of Norwegians, we decided on Nortraship. From that moment, we never had a home for five years. We had a ship to live on."

In 1941, Harry came to Liverpool and met his future wife Mildred, in Linacre Lane, Bootle. "She met me with a friend who thought I was a sheep farmer. I said 'Do you like to see my sheep?' And she ran home! Next month, I met her again. I don't know why I fell in love, but I did."

The couple married on 3 July 1943 in St Matthew's Church, Bootle. He was wearing his Royal Norwegian Navy uniform and she was in white. In true wartime spirit, they stood before the gasworks for the wedding photographs. "The wife always said, 'You have been gassing ever since'," he admitted. Mildred and Harry, who became a painter and decorator after the war, have a daughter, Astrid.

"I have had a wonderful life. I think down the memories of the friends I have had and their comradeship which you never get today," said Harry, who was a marine later in the war and took part in raids in northern Norway.

On his first visit to Liverpool, Harry was mugged, but since then he has crossed words with only one person. "A girl said, 'You shouldn't be living here, you dirty foreigner.' I told her that I was living here before she was born. She knew nothing about me. That hurt me. But the people of Liverpool, especially those around the docks, are the best, the real people."

Most of the sailors enlisted in Nortra immediately after their country's collapse. But stoker, Olaf Oen, returned to his native country, then sailed to the Shetland Islands with ten men and two women. He signed up with the Royal Norwegian Navy and survived the sinking of two ships in the North Atlantic before serving on the *Buttercup*, carrying troops and supplies for the Normandy landings. "I very much resented what the Germans had done to our country," he said.

Unlike most of his comrades, Olaf already had a British bride. In 1937, he had married Kathleen after meeting her in Madame Dennett's dance hall near New Brighton. They still meet their old friends in the church to talk over the old days.

Hilary Ness was secretary of the Norwegian War Veterans' Association for the 20 years before it closed. "There are more widows than veterans now," she said. Her husband, Arvid, who died 26 years ago, was on the convoys. "He was the radiographer and second-mate on a ship which was attacked by a U-boat," she said. "He was going up the ladder to the bridge, the explosion of another ship nearby keeled my husband's ship over and knocked my husband right down on to the iron deck and he got a head injury which kept him semi-conscious for many days."

The couple met in 1943 at the Anglo/Norwegian Society, which met in the British Council's offices in Church Street, Liverpool. They married the following year. "He was absolutely stunning," she said, "a typical Norwegian Viking type, very tall, about six foot three inches. We just fell for each other right away. It was like some sort of chemistry. We felt that we had known each other forever." Arvid was posthumously awarded the King Haakon Medal for his service on the convoys.

Now, every week, about 30 elderly Norwegian men and their Liverpool 'brides' meet in the church for a chat about the old times, a smorgasbord, a couple of prayers and a couple of hymns. Soon, they will be eating in style in the Empire Room of the Adelphi Hotel, Liverpool, at the invitation of the Norwegian Ambassador, Tarald Brautaset. In the evening, he is attending a concert from the Vale Royal String Orchestra, being given in honour of the Norwegian sailors at the Swedish Church. So the spirit of friendship continues between two seafaring peoples.

The name Scouse, of course, is a shortening of the Norwegian lobscouse, a type of stew.

JOHN SHARKEY PRESSES ON

After this article was published in September 2002, I met John at a ceremony to honour Japanese prisoners of war, and he was still pressing on.

~

John Sharkey's trouble was his cool way of looking at a man. He had learned to do this in a tough neighbourhood. With a single dark glance, he could tell you exactly what he thought. This was fine in the jazz bands for which he blew the sweetest trumpet in town – a sinewy figure under his black hire suit and bow-tie. It served him well, too, on the streets, which he had walked bare-foot in the snow as a child, and in the boxing-ring, where his fists were as fast as a pair of wasps in a jar.

But the guards in the Japanese PoW camp didn't like the way John looked at them. They felt the contempt in the unshifting blue of his stare. So they tried to knock it out of him with their fists and boots and clubs. John, the boy from Conway Street in the Everton district of Liverpool, always held his ground, even when he was down. That was the way he had been raised by his mother, Sarah, and father, Daniel, a traction engine driver on a low wage.

The guards even hung him by his thumbs and wrists from the ceiling for hours at a time. He opens his hands, a little veined by the years, to show where they secured the string. Twice the young jazz trumpeter was put in a black steel-box with a slit for air. They left him in the heat of the sun for two days to cook, like a bird in an oven, but he fell out alive, ready for another day of toil, burying dead comrades under the sleepers of the Burma Railway.

"Press on," he said yesterday at his flat not far from his family's old home. "Press on, that's what you had to do."

And the courage has stayed with him. When the doctors discovered a tumour in his stomach earlier this year, they wondered if John would be strong enough for surgery. After all, he was 88, and he seemed a little frail. It might be better just to let events take their course. But this was the army boxing champion they were talking about, the man who had shrugged at Afghan snipers on the North West Frontier. He had been shot in the back and left arm by the Luftwaffe when the British Expeditionary Force was retreating to Dunkirk. John fell in a ditch and woke up again in a Sunderland hospital. The doctors said then that he had taken enough and offered him a medical discharge. He gave them his look. His brothers, Dave, Sam, Bill, Fred and Walter, were all serving their country, he said. So John returned to action in time for the fall of Singapore and imprisonment.

All that happened more than 60 years ago, and earlier this year, he was in the hands of the doctors again. This time, they were talking about removing two-thirds of his stomach. It would take more than three hours, if all went well. John smiled to himself and whispered, "Press on".

The operation was successful, but he had to stay in hospital for two months. Now he is home again, surrounded by his sons and daughters, Edith, Norman, Joan, Ronnie and Val. "When he came in for tests, he looked such a tiny chap," said Mr Peter McCulloch, consultant surgeon at University Hospital, Aintree. "But he's a very tough, spirited individual. It is very unusual to do this operation on someone of that age."

John, who worked in electronics at Plessey's (now Marconi) after the war, lost his wife Edith two years ago. He won't say this himself because he is too modest but, surely, he is the bravest man in Britain.

As a boy, John had the gift of blowing a trumpet in the style of the American jazzmen. Musicians said he had good lips. On leaving Penrhyn Street School, he played for the Modernaires at venues like St Martin's Hall, where couples jitterbugged beneath shimmering silver orbs. The money was good, 12 shillings and sixpence (62p) a night. With the hungry thirties closing in, a career in the Army seemed a safer bet. John trained as a boy soldier, growing rapidly from 4ft 11in to almost 5ft 6in.

Skills in radio communications, coding and cryptography led him into the Signals Corps and long spells overseas, including his brushes with the tribesmen on the North West Frontier. Then came World War II.

John described a beating he had received from Japanese guards who wanted some information. "It didn't do us a lot of good," he said with masterly understatement, as sorrow filled the eyes of his daughter, Val Mullowney, and her daughter, Cathy. Sergeant John Sharkey didn't tell the Japanese anything except his number, 22322130. On the railway, his weight was halved to less than five stone and the smiling Japanese said they were sending him to a copper mine in Formosa for a 'rest'. Conditions were worse.

Then, on 6 August 1945, John heard something strange.

"Everything went black," he recalled. "About five seconds after, there was a big flash and we could feel the earth move." They didn't know the atomic bomb had been dropped on Hiroshima.

He was close to death. After liberation, he needed to be treated for eight months in Canada. John knows he would have died had it not been for his upbringing. He was strong at football, rugby, athletics and boxing, becoming the British Army and International Services featherweight champion. He would comfort and encourage the softer men, but they slipped away. John is not one for boasting. But he admits he was "a very fast fighter". Obviously, he wanted to hit the gloating guards, hard and quick, but discipline was crucial if you wanted to survive the camps. And, of course, that spirit of pressing on. "I wouldn't bend to the Japs," he said. "They didn't like me and I didn't like them. They could see it in my face, the way I looked at them."

ATHOLL DUNCAN'S
LITTLE PIECE OF HISTORY

This article first appeared in January 2002.

It was the rainy season on the island, humid and sullen. Sweat stained the shirts of the soldiers as they huddled under the ceiling fans that whirred away the final days of colonial rule with slow, lazy revolutions.

Everyone sensed something big was about to happen. The old order was changing. Singapore had fallen three weeks before. Now they awaited the fate of Java. But the young captain already had the answer, written on five sheets of paper, hidden in the lining of the glengarry, worn proudly at the angle favoured by the men of the Argyll and Sutherland Highlanders.

Andrew Atholl Duncan knew he had been the messenger at a decisive moment in the history of a world, fast-sinking into chaos and cruelty. As the senior cipher officer, he had decoded the message for General Sitwell who was commanding the British soldiers garrisoned on Java to help the Dutch defend their colony against the Japanese invasion. The message gave the humiliating terms just accepted by Holland. [1.] Unconditional surrender. [2.] All hostilities must immediately cease. [3.] Hoist white flag as sign of capitulation …

Atholl, then 23, asked the stenographer to, "shove in" a carbon so he could have a copy. This was strictly against the rules, but such things didn't matter anymore.

Now, his daughter, Meg Parkes, is reading again the typed document lying on the table in the lounge of her home in Hoylake. Beside it is his glengarry. Both will be shown in an exhibition of his papers and wartime possessions to coincide with the 60th anniversary of the fall of Singapore. It is also the date of publication of her book, *Notify Alec Rattray* … which tells the remarkable story of Atholl and his fiancée, Elizabeth Glassey.

The couple met at a Saturday 'hop' in 1937 at St Andrew's University, Scotland, where he was an engineering student and she was a medical student. Soon they were in love. It was to become an extraordinary romance, always sustained by the faith they had, one for the other. Atholl had joined the university's Officer Training Corps. He went to France with the British Expeditionary Force in 1940 and was evacuated from Cherbourg during the rapid German advance. By January 1942, Atholl was stationed in Singapore as an intelligence officer. His knowledge of ciphering resulted in him being promoted from 2nd lieutenant to captain.

With Singapore's fall, the British HQ was transferred to Lembang in the hills of Java. "Dad was on duty late at night when the Dutch sent a message through to General Sitwell," said Meg. "In later years, he would always smile when he told that story."

She believes that knowing he had a little piece of world history in his hat kept him alive in the Japanese PoW camps. Meanwhile, Elizabeth was continuing her studies, wondering about her man.

Atholl and four of his comrades, calling themselves the 'Five Aces', remained on the run in southern Java for several weeks before being taken prisoner. He had begun writing a diary, which speaks of how the brave spirits of ordinary men can survive, unbowed, in the most appalling circumstances. As well as daily events, Atholl recorded the names and addresses of fellow prisoners and details of what you could do and where you could eat in British cities – anything to keep his mind keen. He would barter cigarettes and his few possessions with other prisoners and 'friendly' Japanese guards for the pens and paper. Meg donated a transcript of the diaries to the Imperial War Museum in London. It forms the basis of her book.

Meg draws attention to the sense of 'captivity' felt by her mother, Elizabeth, who was waiting in the hope that one day she would see her man smile again and run her fingers through his hair. In the summer of 1942, Elizabeth received a bundle of all the letters she had sent to Atholl, all undelivered. "She was devastated that the letters she had been writing every other day had not reached him," said Meg. "She worried about whether he would come back, and if he did, what shape would he be in? She had absolute certainty that she would wait for him, though the strain was almost unbearable."

Atholl was in four Japanese camps, where they dug for coal or farmed. His weight fell to 6st 7lb. Elizabeth finally heard of Atholl's fate through his expatriate friend, Alec Rattray. Fellow prisoner, Sergeant George Armstrong, had broadcast to his Montana home on the Japanese propaganda radio. Part of his message read: 'Notify Alec Rattray of San José, California, that AA Duncan is OK." This was relayed to her.

Atholl and Elizabeth married in January 1946. He returned to university, switching courses to medicine. They had four girls. The couple went into practice together in Hoylake, where they were known as Dr and Mrs Duncan, despite her qualifications. They died within a few days of each other in 1997.

LEARN FROM ME

This piece was first printed in October 1998
following the release of the film *Schindler's List*.

A small pensioner in a fawn mac, just a face lost in the crowd, walked into the picture palace yesterday to tell the children how it was for her family in those days. How, by the flick of a thumb, she was parted forever from her mother, as smoke rose from the death camp chimneys.

Inside, the pupils had returned to their seats after the intermission in *Schindler's List*. Esther Brunstein was in an adjacent auditorium, also in near darkness, to tell journalists how the movie may touch future generations with just a little of the truth. To that extent, it served a purpose. That is why this woman was in the Plaza Cinema on a shopping street in Crosby, speaking of Auschwitz where Jews and social rejects were gassed in four chambers, each of which could hold 6000 people at a time. The young Esther Zylberberg, as she was called then, and her mother Sara were among the thousands of Jews rounded up in the ghetto at Lodz and herded on to cattle trucks.

"When we arrived in Auschwitz, we didn't know what place we were coming to. I cannot tell you to this day whether the journey actually took twelve hours, twenty-four, or forty-eight, or even more," she said. "There were many dead on arrival.

"When we arrived, the people who worked there ..." she paused for long seconds. " ...We looked at them and said, 'Where are we?' They said, 'You're in Auschwitz. Just look there. Can't you see the smoke? That is probably where you will end up.'

"It was just a movement of the thumb," she said. "Right and left. Right meant that you just disappeared. It was death. Left, it meant life, life just for a while. I wanted to follow my mother, but I was pushed back."

They never saw each other again.

The film was almost over. Mrs Brunstein went for a cup of tea before addressing the children from Hugh Baird College, St Wilfred's High School, Savio High School, Deyes High School, St George of England High School and Hillside High School. They had seen Steven Spielberg's film about Oskar Schindler, the German industrialist who conspired to save 1,100 Jews working in his factory from the concentration camps. It was no ordinary showing. The event was organised by the Anti Nazi League, Unison and the Crosby Community Cinema, which runs the Plaza. They hoped that the children, all aged over 15, would learn something of the Holocaust from the film, before they heard Mrs Brunstein's story.

Esther, her parents Philip and Sara, and brothers Peretz and David, lived in the Polish city of Lodz. Anti-Semitism was endemic in Lodz, but it had been possible for the Jews, who accounted for about one third of the 750,000 population, to live in comparative safety. Then Hitler and his Panzer divisions crushed the country's heroic resistance.

"The city was called the Polish Manchester. Weaving was the predominant trade," Esther explained. "Before the outbreak of war, it was the second biggest Jewish community in Europe after Warsaw.

"My father was an active member of a Jewish Socialist organisation. He was a trade unionist, at one time an official. Both brothers were in the youth movement of this party. Even the kindergarten I attended was a creation of this movement. I looked back very fondly on my childhood, even though it was difficult to live in

Poland as a Jewish child. But I had a happy home background, which compensated for the ills outside."

At the beginning of the war, her father and elder brother fled because of the family's political background. Neither survived. The rest of the family were forced into the ghetto where they managed to exist until its liquidation in 1944. Sixteen-year-old Esther and her mother were taken to Auschwitz.

"My mother did not survive, I cannot really talk about it in detail. Suffice it to say that she did not pass selection for life. She was only forty-four years old. I was left on my own. I cannot remember to this day how long I was in Auschwitz. It must have been a matter of weeks because when you start to think about it, you wonder whether it was actually possible to survive.

"I'm just running. It was a time out of mind. It was not a time for thinking. It was living on another planet. It was horrendous. There were eight hundred of us in a block and the first greeting we had from the woman who was in charge was, 'Don't you know you have come here to die? None of you will get out'. This was more or less the life in Auschwitz. It did not belong to the normal way of thinking. It was so inhuman, so horrendous, that people's imaginations cannot take it in. Everyone was deranged. I was witness to a world that was temporarily unhinged.

"What saddens me is that young people are not educated enough, though I understand now that it is on the curriculum. The survivors didn't talk, not because it was their choice, but because it was a taboo subject. People didn't want to know and it is important to know.

"The predominant thought for me was that some of us had to survive. We had to tell the world, or they would never know or believe. We had to. And then, when we did survive, they didn't want to know."

That is why she believes education to be so important and why she continues to talk to people like the audience at yesterday's showing of *Schindler's List*.

"We are getting much smaller in number. I am not a very young person, but I am one of the young ones who survived. This is the main reason why I speak up. Young people should not be indifferent. You must speak up when you feel strongly about it. If you can't do anything physical – scream, shout."

From Auschwitz, Esther was chosen for a labour camp near Hanover. "The man in charge there was the embodiment of evil," she said. "There were four hundred women, but it was better than Auschwitz. We each had a bunk, but conditions were harsh and hard. We stayed there until the camp was liquidated in January 1945. Then we were marched to Belsen, with all the associations which that word has. We were liberated by the British."

Can there be any forgiveness for what happened?

"We are talking about something which was a sophisticated, organised, methodically-run death factory. Those who were left alive were only there for as long as they could make use of them. I can never forgive the perpetrators, never, not those who were actively engaged. To this day, I cannot understand anyone working in the death factory – killing people, gassing people, and they were fathers and brothers and sisters and lovers. How could they sit down in the evening and perhaps write a loving letter home? I can't make sense out of it. I can't forgive them."

After liberation, Esther moved to England and married Stanislav Brunstein, another refugee. They had two daughters.

As she left the auditorium she was approached by Dorothee Smith (née Nussbaum) from Wavertree. They began speaking in Yiddish. Dorothee, a Latvian, had also been separated from her family in the war. There wasn't any hope really, but had Esther heard anything of her little sister Gitta? She would be 65 now, but they never knew what happened to each other.

The sorrow isn't over yet.

As they milled out of the auditorium into the foyer, the children could be heard to be saying that we shouldn't forget. The same words were on all their lips.

Sian McCulloch, head of history at Hillside High School, said: "We are studying Nazi Germany in great detail, and the treatment of Jews and other minorities. This helps them to understand why we should treat minorities in this country in a better way. If they see what happened to the Jews, then maybe next time they see any racist attacks being made, it will make them stand up for what they have been taught about the Holocaust and how its implications are so awful."

ORDINARY PEOPLE,
EXTRAORDINARY LIVES

Fame can be a fine thing and it certainly has its place, but my pleasure has been in drawing the details and stories from the lives of people who are sometimes dismissed as 'ordinary'. What an insult that is to their bravery and talent, their style and essential goodness. In a way, I have been trying to find true celebrity, far away from the TV cameras and glossy magazines. Often I found it. This is a selection of people who had great stories to tell, though they had never seen their names in lights.

A VISIT FROM THE ROCKETMAN

This article appeared in March 1999
when Steve Bennett came to Merseyside to test his latest rocket.

The rocketman with his frizzy beard, three O Levels, and a hard white hat had enough faith to fill a cathedral. He began the countdown from ten to blast-off from his bunker of sandbags in the dunes. Members of the huge media posse watched from a distant rise, swept by a merciless, northerly wind, and gazed at the beach where the little 14ft rocket stood, waiting for her rubber-based solid propellant to be ignited and release 1,100 pounds of thrust. Steve Bennett pushed the red button. Then, for five seconds, stretching to an eternity … nothing happened …

Sadness touched the stare of his devoted wife Adrienne, waiting in her sunrise-orange anorak and foam-headed microphones to broadcast news of Britain's latest space adventure on TV and radio. Then, above the launch pad near the shoreline, flames suddenly raged from the rocket's tail. In his bunker, 50 metres down the coast, Steve's triumphant spring almost made it a double take-off.

This may have been a small step for mankind, but it was a giant leap for the former toothpaste tester whose ambition is to claim the $10m being offered by the American Exprize Foundation to the first non-governmental organisation to launch three people into space.

For all of 18 seconds, the little white tube, called *Tempest*, cut a vapour trail through the air covering half a mile, eventually being lost in cloud as it reached its apogee. Then the black parachute opened perfectly and the rocket, which had touched 700mph, began to descend slowly over the Mersey Estuary at the Altcar Military Range, near Formby.

"Daddy's done it!" said his eight-year old son, Max Bennett. Everyone was cheering, some with relief.

In many ways, this was the perfect, very British story about a glorious eccentric. Dan Dare meets Eddie the Eagle, thanks to Heath Robinson – that's the way the cynics were talking about it. It was also a story of one man's belief, expertise and determination.

The *Tempest's* £3000 voyage was a crucial stage in the development of Steve's Starchaser project. He was testing out the technology needed for flights and recovery over the sea. It meant that his company, Starchaser Ltd, can continue with plans to carry three people 62 miles into the sky. His success has regained for Steve some of the credibility he lost a year ago when the 22-ft Starchaser 3 crashed and burst into flames on Dartmoor after reaching just 200 feet of what should have been a 15,000-ft flight.

In the tense minutes before he retired to the bunker yesterday, Steve, the 34-year-old director of the Space Technology Laboratory at Salford University, said, "One of the problems we have got is the higher you go with a rocket, the bigger the recovery area. If you go more than four miles up anywhere in the UK, the recovery area is going to be so big that we will encroach on populated areas. So it really screws us for launching in the UK, but if you can launch over the sea, you have a massive recovery area. It makes sense to do that. We are testing our technology for making that happen."

Manchester's Air Traffic Control experts restricted the *Tempest's* altitude to 3000ft so that it couldn't interfere with other flights. Even so, the insurance for yesterday's flight was £600 with an indemnity of £1m. As the wind whipped across the undulating mounds of sand, loosely bound by marram grass, it was difficult to see what could be damaged on this stretch of coast used by the military for exercises. To the left was Bootle, with the hills of North Wales barely visible across the water. Nonetheless, all emergency services had been alerted and TA vehicles and personnel (156 Transport Regiment and 238 Squadron) were on the sands, at the ready.

The *Tempest* had been made from a composite material including fibreglass and aluminium and weighs only 50lb. As five launch controllers carried out a final examination, mobile phones trilled from the sand-hills to centrally-heated offices in London. Lift off, scheduled for 10am, had been delayed, and ominously, the winds were gusting at up to 20 knots. Any higher and the whole thing would have been cancelled.

Could it really be called a space flight? "No, no," said Steve, from Duckinfield, Cheshire. "You have to get up to a hundred kilometres for it to be actually called space. This is nowhere near that, but it is going to be a very spectacular firework. We are trying to open the space frontier for the UK. It is a low-level flight but we are testing important technology which will enable us to go to much greater altitudes."

As the rescheduled lift-off approached, Steve was only too aware that it was becoming a PR exercise. "You lot are going to bury us if it doesn't work," he said to a cluster of reporters, before heading for his bunker.

Surely there is a great romance in all this, rattling the gates of Tomorrow? "When I was four years old, I was into Gerry Anderson's *Thunderbirds* and that sort of thing," says Steve, who sees himself as a flesh and blood Thunderbird puppet. "I knew that they were only puppets and it wasn't real, but I wanted to make it real. I wanted to bring it alive and that's what I am doing.

"Okay, I am not rescuing puppets in distress and stuff like that, but I want to open the space frontier. I love *Star Trek*. I love the idea of going to distant planets. We are many years away from that, sending people to Mars and stuff, but I want to do my bit to make it happen. Now we are working on a rocket that carries people into space. We are building a mock-up of it now. We are going to have a prototype flight pretty soon. Ten million dollars are up for grabs if you can launch three people up one hundred kilometres. We are going after that. We'll make a lot of money doing it and it will be a lot of fun. I'm coming out of the closet now. I want to be in that capsule."

With such determination and faith, the boy who left Egerton Park Secondary School, Denton, with O Levels in Chemistry, Physics and Art, may well achieve his ambition.

The next project of Steve and Adrienne, who have a two-year-old daughter Tabetha, as well as Max, is to launch the 21-ft Starchaser 3A to 120,000 feet. For the more ambitious programme leading to the manned flight, Steve is looking at sites in Russia and the USA. Max added, "At first I thought everything was going to go wrong, but he's made it."

Steve strode to the cameras with arms aloft. "Everything worked out exactly as planned. We worked it all out in the lab. But there is nothing like bringing it out into the field and putting the rocket through its paces to make sure you've got your sums right. It looks like we know what we are doing.

"I had a job to do. Up to pressing that button, I just got on with it, but after pressing it, you start worrying. Then the rocket goes and you can let your emotion out. You can collapse in a heap, shout or jump about. Out of ten launches we have done, eight have been successful. So that's not bad. Even NASA loses rockets.

"I have dreamed of moments like this all my life. It's what gets me through the difficult times. You know, when you are banging your head against a brick wall, trying to get someone to give you a can of paint to finish the launch pad."

So the man who once tested toothpaste for bacteria, walked away on firm ground, thinking of the stars.

THE MAN WHO SAVED LIVES

The story of Jim Clarke, a gentle giant. First printed in January 2002.

He came to the city as a stranger, a bewildered and hungry stowaway on a cargo boat, missing the warmth of his home in South America. When he died, hundreds lined the streets in silent respect, remembering the big man with the deep voice, who sang lullabies and spirituals as he handed out the peanuts he had gathered from the docks for the children to roast over their fires at home. Some of those children still rest flowers on the grave of Jim Clarke in thanks for saving their lives when they were drowning in the Leeds and Liverpool Canal.

In those days, the boys and girls swam in a stretch of the canal known as the 'scaldies' because it was heated by the boiling water that flushed into the canal after it had been used in the refining process at the Tate and Lyle sugar factory. These were pale children, often suffering from chronic chest conditions. You could be hard on the street with your swagger and stare and almost completely helpless in the water. Nobody then kept a tally of the numbers hauled to safety by the strong hands of Jim, but it ran into dozens.

Jim came to the city in 1900, hidden on a ship carrying timber. The reasons for his leaving Georgetown, British Guiana (now Guyana) as a shy 14-year-old, were never fully explained. A superstitious man, all he told his children was that a fortune-teller had warned him something bad would happen if he didn't leave his native country.

Liverpool was a glamorous, expanding port, but big places can be lonely. Jim was found wandering the streets by Benedictine priests from St Augustine's Church on Great Howard Street. They offered him food and shelter at their presbytery while lodgings were arranged with a local family.

Black people had not settled in that part of the city, so Jim, who was already more than 6ft, immediately attracted attention. With his gentle manner, ready smile and athletic potential, he soon made friends, though.

It was thought Jim would be a boxer as he could weave and dance, duck, dive and punch with a speed that dazzled those tough young men in the neighbourhood who fancied themselves with their fists. At just over 12 stone, he had the taut, muscular build of a real contender. Indeed, he sparred with some leading fighters. But he was not by nature inclined to hurt others. Instead, swimming became his sport and he developed breathing exercises that enabled him to stay underwater for long periods. His potential was spotted at the Wavertree Swimming Club where he won numerous medals between 1908-1910. He also raced with the Bootle, Waterloo, and Everton Swimming clubs, bringing in the honours.

Jim was invited by Liverpool Police to coach their swimming and boxing teams. By then, he was a docker and the emergency services were always informed of his whereabouts in case they needed him to help with a rescue. His medals and certificates for bravery date back to 1911 and were issued by, among others, the police and the Liverpool Shipwreck and Humane Society. Jim also saved colleagues who had fallen into the docks. His ability to swim underwater meant that he had to recover bodies. Saddened by these experiences, he taught schoolchildren how to swim at the nearby Burroughs Gardens Baths.

Aside from serious swimming, Jim created a compelling act in which he sang songs such as *My Darling Clementine* underwater with a bucket over his head. His voice rose to the surface with a melody and tone imitating his hero Paul Robeson.

Jim married Elizabeth Murphy in 1914 in the Church of Our Lady of Reconciliation in Eldon Street. They set up home in Elizabeth Terrace and had 13 children, eight of whom survived into adulthood. The family then moved to Ashfield Cottages in Blenheim Street. Three of the children are still alive: Vincent, 65, and the twins Winnie and Michael, 69.

Jim died in 1946, aged 60. His funeral was held at St Sylvester's Church and he was buried at Ford Cemetery. A street in the area is named after him, but otherwise he is one of Liverpool's great unsung heroes.

Terry Cooke, a local writer and group chairman of the Vauxhall History and Heritage Group, remembers Jim. "I remember, as a child, seeing children running along the cobbles towards Jim's house," he said. "We knew somebody would be in the canal. Jim never accepted credit for what he had done, though we know he saved a lot of children, dockers and seaman. Even now people remember him coming back from the docks with pockets full of nuts."

The Vauxhall History and Heritage Group and the local people of Vauxhall from around the old streets off Scotland Road, are planning a memorial plaque to him, to be made by Fred O'Brien, an architectural designer. It will be a recognition of how an outsider came to be loved in the community as a life-saver, a boxer, a swimmer, an entertainer, a husband, a father and a storyteller. More than all those things, though, Jim was a humble gentleman, with God in his heart. To his son, Vincent, he was simply a lovely man, a father who sang: "Oh, my baby, my curly-headed baby."

THE INVENTOR

An invitation to enter the studio and mind of inventor Jim Baxter
and see the place where dreams come to life. First printed November 2001.

On the hour, the chiming of the clocks quite overwhelms the soft Edinburgh tones
of this tall man. He is crouching on the lounge carpet to demonstrate his miniature
Chinese chariot, which always points to the south. You feel at once there is
inventive genius in this man in the checked shirt, who has scattily knotted his tie
so that the thin end is longer than the wide end.

In a brick studio a few yards away, vampire bats and spiders hang motionless
over his vintage Lancia racing car. A pretty girl with a watering-can stands still
between the flowers beds, a witch stares into her brew, and a trout is frozen in
mid-leap. They all await the touch of Jim Baxter, whose fingers first gave them
'life'. He calls his work 'mechanical and innovative engineering', but in this
soulless time of technology and mass production, Jim plucks dreams from his
head and offers them to others.

Take, for example, the clock that he made from a dustbin lid, which ticks in the
café of the Victorian Palm House in Sefton Park. Jim likes clocks. He builds them
and restores them. There is a clock in his shed that he fashioned from bike chains,
pulleys and sprockets. Given the circumstances of its conception, it keeps
reasonably good time, losing about 15 seconds a week. Jim's the sort of chap who
can lose a few seconds without worrying unduly. He could never be a slave to

punctuality. That is not his style. Life is rich in its surprises, not in its certainties.

Near the clock are flamingos, the teapot and the Cheshire Cat from Alice's Adventures in Wonderland. Jim is the maker of wonders. Some might call them automata, but that would be to miss the romance of their creation. Behind his work, there shines a faith. He expresses it simply:

"I am just a practical man who has the benefit of not having had a good education. I am my own man. Consequently, I have no theory of a school-room nature. I have practical knowledge, but no theory. You get the young man who goes to university, studies engineering and does very well, getting all the theory in the world, but he won't get enough practice. I feel that, anyway," he explains.

Jim is 70 years old and lives with his wife, Jane, in a hidden house on the outskirts of Liverpool. For nine years they were among those who campaigned and worked for the restoration of the Palm House in Sefton Park. Its reopening last month was a shared dream come true. To mark that occasion he made a frame around the commemorative cake, from which he dangled a spider. It symbolised the webs spun across the glass-house during its long years of neglect.

"The nice thing is that people in this city come to me with odd bits and pieces," Jim says. "Several firms call me when they want something special making. I have sentiment in my work. I am dedicated to this privilege that I have been given, of being able to repair things."

Earlier this month he completed a commission to build nine stands for musicians in the Royal Philharmonic Orchestra. It was a more conventional task but, as always, his application to the job was absolute.

Like so many Scotsmen, Jim had an affinity with engineering and the great engineers of past generations. By the age of 13, he was working in a garage. His family came to Liverpool from Scotland after the end of World War II. Jim's passion then was for cars and motorbikes, particularly those built by Italian engineers, whose innovative skills he rates very highly. He still rides a motorbike, a 1929 Scott at the moment. "She runs extremely well," he says. "I like motorbikes, particularly British and Italian ones."

For five years, Jim ran his own museum of transport, automata, and strange inventions, in Lark Lane, Liverpool, but it closed 12 years ago. Some of the exhibits were transferred to the Williamson Museum, Birkenhead, where they are still on display.

What about this miniature Chinese chariot with the pointer on its top? It was a development from the days of engineering's infancy. Now Jim has made his version, as a toy for his five grandchildren. "The Chinese wanted to explore the northern reaches of their country for lots of reasons," he says. "But they kept getting lost, so the emperor decreed that they should make a mechanical device that would enable them to come back home safely. It was called the south-pointing chariot and bits of it were found in the tomb of the thousand warriors. They were a very clever people, the Chinese, and for the metal parts they used bronze, but they cast the gears in china (pottery). That was between two and three thousand years ago. This is just a mock-up, a bit of fun."

Jim is reluctant to remove the top to show why the pointer is always southward, irrespective of the vehicle's direction. It's a secret between him and the ancient Chinese.

Although his work is brilliant, the charm lies in a quirkiness sure to appeal to children. Jim gives talks and demonstrations at local schools. "People are immediately intrigued when you change the scale of something," he says. In a demonstration of leverage, he shows the pupils how a see-saw works, requiring them to make their own little ones. "It brings merriment to them," he says. "At one school we had forty see-saws going down the corridor, laid one over the over, so they went down domino-style."

Jim wanders into his studio. Overhead is the giant spider. It starts to move up and down on a long, thick strand. "Oh, my God!" I say.

"Everybody always says that. Everybody, without exception," Jim says. "When the vicar came, I told him I was doing a lot for religion because everyone who sees the spider uses those three words. She's the true Maud." I look bemused and repeat the name. "That's what we call her," Jim explains. "Moves Automatically Up and Down."

The spider is powered by seven battery-powered motors and a compressor. Among her many tricks, she lights up her eyes, drinks from a can of cola, makes a rude noise, and blows a party whistle. Behind her, we have a witch stirring her potion, the girl watering the garden, and an angler casting his line as the trout jumps. The studio defies description with its clocks, motorised scooters (specially built for World War II parachutists), bats, insects, bikes and clown. It must have been a place of enchantment for his children, Barry and Annmarie.

Presently, Jim is working on the restoration of a seventeenth century Dutch clock, believed to be one of the first to be operated by the long pendulum. "This gives me great, great pleasure," he says. "I feel privileged to be able to work on it.

"I am into the psychology of making things. I love my work, I just love it. I live for it," Jim says. "I like to make things that other people wouldn't want to make because it is not quite their thing. When I work, I go into a bit of a trance. You have to be utterly involved in what you are doing. I can always put a bit extra in to make something better. There is always the best way of doing something, if you think it out. My son says, 'You only taught me one thing, Dad. You taught me how to think.'

"I do seem to be privileged with my delightful friends, most of them near in age to me. We have all been through similar experiences. I am married to a lovely wife who aids and abets me in everything I do. In fact, she takes a practical interest and helps me out physically with a lot of the jobs."

Jim leaves the room. All is still again. For him, there is the world of wonder and the world outside. It starts to rain as he stands, smiling, by the door to his dreams.

THE CAMPAIGNERS

Swept along by the frenzy of Spanish bullfighters, three brave friends from Southport try to catch the cruelty on film to dissuade politicians from supporting the barbarity with EU subsidies. This article was first printed in September 2002.

~

Young Morenito the bull was bred to be brave. This way, his last minutes on earth would make a grand spectacle. He didn't know that. How could he, grazing and snorting in his field with the other bulls? Then, one day, strange men came with a truck to take him away from all that he had ever trusted. Morenito was being offered as a gift from one people to another, from the people of Hagetmau in France to its twin town, Tordesillas. It was a mark of the respect held between them. Of course, Morenito didn't know anything about that either, though instinctively he felt wary and nervous.

There was a look of bewilderment in his big eyes when the crazy boys from the strangers' town chased and poked him down the stone street over the bridge to the place where it was to happen. There, in a field, they were waiting, some on stallions, others on foot. A few of them carried lances, each about 12 feet long and tipped at the end with spearheads like those that had been used in mediaeval battles. These men and boys began stabbing his sleek black coat until the blood changed Morenito's colour. They were shouting and making gestures with their hands, urging him to put on a good show, to please the crowd, but the bull was alone and frightened.

He began running towards the pine wood at the end of the field and the men in front of him fell back, mocking him and laughing. Their taunts became louder, particularly from those drinking red wine straight from the bottle. They wanted him to be even braver. The night before, some of them had put him in a cage to stop him struggling as they polished his horns. Anyone who knew anything about bulls could see he wasn't going to use them to charge now. Morenito was trying to get away. All 600 kilograms of him was twisting and turning to find a way through the saplings and the people, where he could escape the noise and the pain, a quiet spot like the field where he had lived before all this started. But the mob was mad.

Among the crowd was Matilda Mench. She felt she was almost inside the bull's spirit as he entered these last moments of life. Her hands were trembling on the video camera and her green eyes were blurred. She felt sick with grief and anger. Yet she knew she must go on filming so that the whole world could see what the people of this town had done to Morenito in celebration of some forgotten virgin from the Christian faith.

The bull didn't sense much after that. He stumbled to the ground as the leading spearmen thrust deep into his heart and vital organs. For Morenito, it was over. It had taken about 20 minutes in the late September morning.

Tony Moore, Matilda's boyfriend, who was taking still photographs, noticed how much smaller the bull looked slumped on the ground with the life passing from his body. Nobody would be frightened of him now.

The mob surged forward. There were about 40,000 of them. They wanted to stand on the bull, all heroes at the killing. There was one who had done more than the others. He was a boy with a swagger and he wore a band in his hair like a warrior. His was the fatal thrust, he claimed. To him belonged the honour. They would raise glasses to his name.

Before that, though, Morenito was hoisted up, to help the ones at the back see what had been done. Then the man who claimed the killing as his own was presented with Morenito's tail and testicles. Later, he would be given the head as well, but removing that was a job for a professional butcher, not the spearmen in the wood.

In the coming weeks, politicians from Spain, Germany, Britain and the European Parliament will see the photographs and films taken by Matilda, Tony and their friend Billy Johnson. The footage shot by Billy, who runs a video shop in Southport, is particularly strong, showing in gory detail what actually happens at these events. They want them to know what happens in the ancient festival of Toro de la Vega (Bull in the Field) in the town of Tordesillas in north western Spain, where they honour the Virgen de la Pena by torturing and killing a fully grown bull.

Matilda and Tony live together at Tony's home in Southport. They run the charity, Fight Against Animal Cruelty in Europe and are also involved with Initiative Anti-Corrida. They hope that their pictures and film will persuade the authorities to ban bullfighting and blood fiestas in Spain. This is not the romance of Ernest Hemingway. It is not a courting ritual for young men with swollen pride. This is barbarity. This is cruelty and it shames human nature.

Tony's late wife, Vikki, spent much of her adult life campaigning against blood sports. She died in February 2000, from a massive haemorrhage, almost certainly the result of being gored by a bull five years earlier when she tried to stop a blood fiesta in Coria near the Portugese border. She was 44. Vikki never blamed the bull.

They think of Vikki, her bravery as a tiny woman facing the big men tormenting the bulls. Vikki will always be with Tony and Matilda because they will always share her dream of ending cruelty to animals. In a way, she was with them still in the Spanish town, filming the killing of Morenito.

As foreigners observing the festival, they were jostled, punched, kicked and verbally abused, but they managed to get their images. "To think we pay for this," says Tony, referring to the EU subsidies from the richer countries, including Britain. The subsidies finance the farmers who breed bulls for ritual torture and death.

Tony holds on to the hope that their evidence will be crucial in their campaign to have bullfighting and blood fiestas banned. In the past, supporters of the festivals have pointed to the importance such events have in the culture of Spain, and to a lesser extent Portugal and France. They argue that the festivals are often linked to religious figures. Additionally, they provide an outlet for the bloated courage of the young men in small towns and villages, and add to the local economy.

Bullfighting in the big rings is heavily promoted by Spain's tourist industry, but outsiders are not welcome at the blood fiestas, which are very much local affairs. Most Spaniards are against them and the numbers of their 'animal activists' are increasing. In fact, at Tordesillas, the head of one activist was paraded on a wanted poster. A recent poll showed that 94 per cent of Spaniards think the fiestas should be stopped. In rural areas, the fiestas remain popular and often enjoy the support of local government.

Tony and Matilda realise the emotional drive of their campaign has to be given a political edge if it is to succeed. They want the bullfights and the fiestas to be outlawed. "Our purpose today was to gather information," says Tony. "We wanted good quality video footage and stills. But we also wanted to speak to the people, so that we can give our testimony from what they told us and what we saw.

"With this information, we are going to spread the word very widely. We are going to the European Parliament in Strasbourg and to our own parliament. We will be speaking to the MEPs of Spain, Britain, Germany and other countries.

"The killing of the bull was the highlight of a fiesta which lasts about two weeks. They all live for it," says Matilda, who was born in Munich. "At twelve thirty, on the night before the killing, the bull is paraded through the streets into the packed bullring, where they have fun with him for half an hour. They dance around him, trying to enrage him. The next morning at eleven, the bull is released and run through the picturesque town and chased into the field."

There comes a bitter twist. If a bull makes it through the pine wood to the border of the town, he is pardoned. It happened in 1995, but the bull's wounds were so bad that he had to be 'humanely' destroyed.

Morenito had no chance of making it. "They were all jumping on him, saying, 'I did it, I did it, me, me, me,'" says Tony. "It was revolting. You have to remember that, before this, he was living in a herd without many people around. From that, he found himself besieged by forty thousand people. There was a look in his eyes of total bewilderment. He was trying to hide. I had this feeling that he wanted to be safe again, in the field where he belonged."